AMONG THE CELESTIALS.

A NARRATIVE OF TRAVELS IN MANCHURIA, ACROSS THE GOBI DESERT, THROUGH THE HIMALAYAS TO INDIA.

ABRIDGED FROM "THE HEART OF A CONTINENT."

BY CAPTAIN FRANCIS YOUNGHUSBAND, C.I.E.,

INDIAN STAFF CORPS,
GOLD MEDALLIST ROYAL GEOGRAPHICAL SOCIETY.
AUTHOR OF "THE HEART OF A CONTINENT," "SOUTH AFRICA OF TO-DAY," ETC.

WITH MAP AND ILLUSTRATIONS.

LONDON:
JOHN MURRAY, ALBEMARLE STREET.
1898.

LONDON:
PRINTED BY WILLIAM CLOWES AND SONS, Limited,
STAMFORD STREET AND CHARING CROSS.

Frontispiece.

IN THE HIMALAYAS.

TO THE MEMORY OF

MY MOTHER,

THROUGH WHOM, AS THE SISTER OF ROBERT SHAW,

I INHERITED THE SPIRIT OF EXPLORATION;

AND TO WHOSE KEEN INTEREST IN ALL MY PLANS,

AND THE

SELF-DENYING ENCOURAGEMENT SHE GAVE ME

IN THEIR EXECUTION,

I OWE SO MUCH OF WHAT SUCCESS HAS ATTENDED MY WORK,

I Dedicate

THIS RECORD OF MY TRAVELS,

PREFACE.

At the close of the journey which this book describes, I was asked to deliver a lecture before the Royal Geographical Society. Being only twenty-four years of age I was not unnaturally in some trepidation at the thought of addressing the greybeards of so scientific a body. But one of them—a hearty old Admiral —gave me a piece of advice which quickly relieved my mind. He said : " Leave out the Geography ! " All the small details important to a Geographer might be published in the official " Proceedings " ; at an evening lecture graphic incidents and personal adventures would be much more appreciated.

In my previous book, 'The Heart of a

Continent,' I endeavoured to give as many of the geographical details I had observed as seemed to me would be of service to geographers and future travellers. In the present I have felt myself at liberty to discard such dry matter and retain only what has some small chance of interesting an overburdened public.

Travellers are not less vain than the rest of mankind—probably more so—and I like to delude myself with the hope that some of my experiences, some account of those remote haunts of nature which I visited as well as of the child-races and historical people whom I met may still be of interest to my countrymen at home. My sincerest wish at any rate is that I may be able to communicate to them even a spark of that keen pleasure and enthusiasm which exploration so amply affords.

For greater convenience I have divided the previous book into two parts. The first dealing with my travels in the Chinese Empire I now publish, and to the original have added a special chapter on the outlook in Manchuria. The second part which describes my travels in the borderland between British and Russian territory in Central Asia will be published under the title ' Between Two Empires.'

F. E. YOUNGHUSBAND.

MOUNT ABU,
  RAJPUTANA, INDIA.
    March, 1898.

CONTENTS.

LIST OF ILLUSTRATIONS.

AMONG THE CELESTIALS.

CHAPTER I.

THE EVER-WHITE MOUNTAIN.

WHAT it was that first started me off on wanderings, which for ten years led me over so large a portion of Asia, it is difficult to say exactly. But I think the first seeds of divine discontent at staying still were sown in the summer of 1884, when I had obtained a few months' leave from my regiment, the King's Dragoon Guards, then stationed at Rawal Pindi, in the Punjab, and made use of it to tour through some of the lower ranges of the Himalayas.

My instinct first led me to Dharmsala, for many years the home of my uncle, Robert Shaw, who, with Hayward, was the first Englishman to push his way through the

Himalayas to the plains of Turkestan beyond. Here I found many of his old pensioners—men who had accompanied him on his several journeys to Yarkand and Kashgar, the principal towns on the northern side of the Himalayas—and books too, and maps, and old manuscripts. I was among the relics of an explorer, at the very house in which his schemes were formed, and from which he had started to carry out his plans. I pored over the books and maps, and talked for hours with the old servants, till the spirit of exploration gradually entered my soul, and I rushed off on a preliminary tour on foot in the direction of Tibet, and planned a great journey into that country for the following year.

That first wild wandering through the Himalayas is one on which I look back with almost keener enjoyment than on any other journey I have subsequently made. I had been in Switzerland and seen snow-mountains before, but only as a boy, when I was not able to wander as I would. Now I was free, and in all the pride and keenness of twenty-one. One march a day was not enough for me; I made two regularly, and sometimes three, and wanted to go everywhere in the two months, which was all I then had available. The scenery of such valleys as those of Kangra and Kulu was enchanting, and then came the excitement of preparing to cross my first snow-pass. I had pictured to myself every imaginable horror from descriptions in books (written, of course, as I afterwards understood, from experiences at exceptional seasons), and I can still recall my disappointment at finding that all these horrors had degenerated down to simple heart-breaking plodding through soft deep snow hour after hour, with an icy wind blowing, and the sun striking down on the top of my head and combining with the rarefaction of the air to give me as bad a headache as I ever had. Then, too, the feeling of disgust and despair at the sight of those bare brown mountains which lie beyond the first forest-clad zone of the Himalayas, their cold and almost repellent appearance, which clearly warns the traveller against entering their rigid clutches—all this I remember well, as well as the rawness and in-experience of the whole of my arrangements, and the discovery that I could not march for twenty or thirty miles a day, as I had imagined

I should be able to do, with just about enough food for the whole day as would form a decent breakfast for a man in hard work. And yet there was a delicious sense of satisfaction as each long day's march was over, as each snowy pass was crossed, each new valley entered, and the magnificent health and strength which came therewith inspired me with the feeling of being able to go anywhere and do anything that it was within the powers of man to do.

From this first tour through the Himalayas I came back with the exploring fever thoroughly on me, and I plunged incessantly into books of travel. But the immediate cause of my first big journey was Mr. James.* It was by the greatest piece of good fortune that we came together. We met first at a dinner-party at Simla, and the conversation between us turned on Yarkand and Kashgar. (I would beg my readers thoroughly to impress upon their minds the position of these places, for their names will frequently be mentioned throughout this book.) I naturally waxed eloquent on the

---

* Mr. H. E. M. James, C.S.I., of the Indian Civil Service, then Director-General of the Post-Office in India, now Commissioner in Sind.

subject, and a week or two afterwards we again met at dinner, and again talked about the same places. And then, after a few days, on one Sunday afternoon, Mr. James walked into my house and asked me if I would go a journey with him. Nothing was said as to where we should go; but to go a journey anywhere was enough for me, and of course I said "Yes." I remember sitting that afternoon in church at Simla and looking up the rows of people, thinking how every man amongst them would wish to be in my place, if he only knew what I was going to do; for at that time I thought that everybody must necessarily want to make a journey if he could only get the chance, and that this must be the highest object of a man's ambition.

Mr. James, it appeared, had originally intended to travel with Mr. Carey, the well-known explorer of Tibet, who was just then starting on his travels. But there had been difficulty about Mr. James's leave, and so he had had to postpone his journey till the following spring, and, being without a companion, had asked me to join him wherever he might go. This act of kindness is one for which

I shall ever be grateful, and I shall always feel that it was to Mr. James that I owe the first start on my career of travel.

Both of us had an inclination towards China, and we at once decided in a general way that to China we should go. It so happened that in my leisure hours I had read up a number of books about Manchuria, Mongolia, and North China, and compiled itineraries from them. I was therefore able to give my chief, Sir Charles Macgregor, then Quartermaster-General in India, some little proof that I was serious in the matter, and he promised to help me and do what he could to smooth over difficulties about my leave.

Our plans now shaped themselves into a journey round Manchuria. It was a country of many interests, and was then but little known. It was the cradle of the present ruling dynasty of China; and the few travellers who had been there had described its lovely scenery, its noble rivers, its fertility and natural resources, and the healthiness of its climate. Reading all this in the heat of India, we were fascinated by such descriptions; and as its proximity to Russian territory on the one hand

and Japan on the other gave it a military and political importance, the extent of which may be even better appreciated to-day than twelve years ago, we felt that time spent in such a country could not possibly be wasted.

On March 19, 1886, we left Calcutta, and early in May found ourselves at Newchwang, the treaty port of Manchuria. This was to be the base of operations, and we were fortunate enough to be joined here by Mr. H. Fulford, of the Chinese Consular Service, an officer who spoke Chinese thoroughly well, knew all the customs of the country, and was able to give us that assistance which as strangers in the land we so much needed.

It is not, however, my intention to give a full detailed account of our journey in Manchuria, for that has already been done by Mr. James in his book, "The Long White Mountain," in which will be found not only a description of our travels, but a fund of information about the history, the religion, and the customs of the people. I shall merely supplement his more important work with a few of the impressions which were left upon me personally.

Our first objective point was a mountain well known in Chinese legends—the Chang-pai-shan, or "Ever-White Mountain." This fabulous mountain had, it is true, been visited in 1709 by one of those enterprising Jesuit surveyors, who seem to have penetrated everywhere and compiled a map of the Chinese Empire remarkable for its accuracy. But no European had subsequently visited the mountain to corroborate their accounts, and much romantic mystery was still attached to it.

The Ever-White Mountain was reported to be situated in the heart of an immense forest, to be of enormous height (the name itself suggesting a snow-clad peak), and to have an unfathomable lake at its summit. We were accordingly fired with enthusiasm to penetrate its mystery and ascend its summit, and on May 19 we left the treaty port of Newchwang with this object in view.

We now had our first taste of Chinese travel, and it proved on the whole by no means unpleasant. In the first place, the climate was perfect—mild and soft, like an English summer. The country was everywhere richly cultivated, and was dotted over with well-built, pent-roofed farmhouses, not unlike those which one sees in England. We travelled in carts—the small carts so often described in books on China—with two mules each, driven tandem, the baggage piled up inside and behind, and ourselves seated at the base of the shafts alongside the drivers, with our legs dangling over the side. In the summer months, when the roads are soft and muddy, the pace is not rapid, and the traveller can jump off, walk alongside, and jump on again as he likes. But in the winter, when the roads are frozen and worn down by the heavy traffic almost as smooth as an asphalte roadway, these carts trundle along at a good five or six miles an hour, and with a thousand or twelve hundred pounds of goods will do their thirty miles a day without any difficulty.

Everywhere along the road are found inns where accommodation for man and beast can be obtained. The first plunge from European civilization—which in our case was represented by the house of Mr. Allen, the British Consul at Newchwang — into a Chinese inn is not agreeable, and the dirt inside and out seems insupportable. But on settling down to the inevitable roughness of travel, one appreciates its many advantages. As a rule a private room can be obtained, the necessaries of life are easily procurable, and fodder for the animals is always ready. These inns are generally well-built houses, and are a real boon to the native travellers and merchants. There is usually one long room, with a low platform on either side and a passage down the middle. On these platforms, or *kangs*, which can be warmed underneath, the guests reclining or squatting at the low tables which are placed on them eat their meals and chat volubly the while. At night the travellers sleep in long rows, cheek by jowl, along the platforms.

At 120 miles from Newchwang we reached Mukden, the capital of Manchuria, and at one time the seat of government of the present reigning dynasty of China. Our reception there was not pleasant, and as we rode through the streets in search of an inn, we were followed even into the house by a hooting, yelling crowd. A Chinaman has no regard for privacy, and these men showed considerable annoyance because we would not let them into our private room, and allow them to stare at us, examine

A MANCHURIAN HOUSE.

Page 10.

everything we possessed, feel our clothes to see what sort of cloth they were made of, and question us unceasingly about our ages, where we had come from, how long we meant to stay, and where we were going. Even when we had cleared our room, they did not desist from pestering us, but, while we were undressing, poked holes with their fingers in the paper windows, and then applied their eyes to these easily-made peep-holes. Looking up in the middle of our ablutions, we would see a mass of eyes—just the eyes, with nothing else visible—peering at us. The effect was peculiarly irritating, and we would dash out with furious remonstrance ; but as soon as we were inside again they would come back exactly as before, and we had eventually to resign ourselves to the inevitable.

But these are the ordinary experiences of every traveller in China, and I am only repeating what has been described a hundred times before. We were kept a week at Mukden, making up a caravan of mules to take us into the mountains. We accordingly had time to see the sights of the place, and go some excursions in the neighbourhood. Of

these the most interesting was to the tomb of
Nurhachu, the founder of the present dynasty.
Manchus have high ideas as to the resting-
places befitting their great men, and there are
few more impressive tombs than this of the
simple mountain chief who raised his clan from
perfect obscurity to be the rulers of the most
populous empire the world has ever seen.
Situated in the country, away from the din of
city life, in the midst of a park of sombre
cypresses many miles in extent, and surrounded by a wall, at the massive gateway
of which guards are placed to prevent any
but Manchus of pure descent from entering,
it impresses the imagination with a sense of
dignified repose, in truest keeping with its
object.

In Mukden, too, and its neighbourhood there
are many temples, but of the ordinary Chinese
type, and of no special interest.   In the matter
of temples, indeed, the Chinese are singularly
unsuccessful in inspiring interest.   I did not
see a single temple in China that really impressed me—not one to compare with those
which may be seen in any part of India.   With
but few exceptions, they are tawdry and even

flimsy, and one never seems to meet with evidence of that immense amount of care and labour and thought in their construction, or of that sense of the beautiful, which characterises the great temples of India. The wooden pillars, often plain, and the grotesquely painted walls which one mostly sees in China, are a poor substitute for the stately marble pillars and exquisite carvings of an Indian temple.

On May 29 our caravan was complete, and we left Mukden to travel eastward to the Yalu river, on the borders of Corea. We soon entered a hilly country, and the scenery daily increased in loveliness—hillsides covered with woods of a thoroughly English type, oaks and elms such as we never see in India, and valleys filled with thriving little villages and hamlets, and streams and rivers affording glimpses of exquisite beauty. The quantity of flowers and ferns too, was extraordinary. Mr. James was making a botanical collection, and in one day we found five different kinds of lily of the valley, maidenhair ferns of various forms—one especially lovely, in shape like a kind of spiral bowl—lilies, violets, anemones, and numbers of other English flowers. We were in a

perfect little country, and we revelled in the
beauties about us.

But beautiful though the country was,
travelling through it was not unattended with
disadvantages, for it rained almost daily at this
season. We fortunately always had either inns
or farmhouses in which to put up at night, but
we were constantly drenched through on the
march, and the going was excessively heavy.
We had work, too, to get over the ground at
the rate we wished. We used to rise at 4.30
or 5 every morning, pack up our things, have
our breakfast, and then have to hang about for
two dreary hours whilst the lazy mule-men were
loading up their animals. On the march we
had to keep constant watch over the mules to
help them past rocky prominences by the river-
side, over boggy places, and through the thick
low scrub of the woods. At midday we halted
for a couple of hours to feed man and beast,
and then went on again till six or seven in the
evening. It was constant, steady work throughout, and more than once on the march I remember being so tired that I lay down on a
fallen log, propped myself up against some
branch, and went off fast asleep in spite of

the rain which was pattering down on the top of me. What I felt particularly, too, at this period was the want of milk and butter, for the Chinese and Manchus never milk their cows, and none was therefore procurable. They seem to think it disgusting to drink milk. They will eat rats and dogs and bird's-nest soup, but they will not drink milk. And we greatly missed this simple necessary, and eventually had to take large quantities of oil with our food in its place.

The heavy rain we were now experiencing naturally swelled the rivers, and a dozen miles from its source a stream would be unfordable. When that is the case, the traveller has either to cross in one of the native "dug-outs"—mere logs of wood with a hollow scooped out down the centre—or wait several days till there is a lull in the flood. This last is what we had to do on more than one occasion, and in some ways I was glad ; for it gave us a little rest and time to overhaul and repair our kit. On such occasions we put up in some farmhouse near the river, and here out in the country, away from the crowds of the towns, we could examine John Chinaman at leisure. All the part we were now in has been colonized by pure Chinese, who are taking the place of the original Manchus. These latter were few in number, and had been drafted off with their families to garrison the towns of China proper, and now the Chinese immigrants from the over-populated or famine-stricken districts of China were flowing into the Manchurian valleys, clearing away the forests, and bringing year by year more land under cultivation. They were, in fact, doing here exactly what our colonists have been working at for so many years in Canada. The amount of work they got through was marvellous. At the first streak of dawn they rose, had a good meal, and then set to at that heart-breaking labour, clearing the ground of the stumps of trees which they had felled. Hour after hour they would toil away, hacking and hewing, and some of them digging up the ground and preparing it for a crop, and at midday they would stop and have another square meal; then return to the same old wearing task till darkness set in when they would come trooping in for their evening repast. They were for the most part strong, hard men, with enormous appetites. Millet porridge, vegetable stews, and soups were their chief food, which they ate out of bowls in huge quantities. Their houses were often comfortable, well-built, and roomy, though not always as clean as they might have been, but still on the whole far better homes than one would expect to find in the backwoods of a colony. And I was struck with the energetic spirit which these colonists showed in pushing their way through the forests. A Chinaman is always known to be industrious, but here was good tough vigour in addition.

At length we reached the Yalu, the natural boundary between Corea and Manchuria. It was a noble river where we struck it—three hundred yards or so broad, and ten to fifteen feet deep. Its sides were covered down to the water's edge with forests, and at intervals, where the ground was flatter, were patches of cultivation and a few farmhouses, or meadows covered with flowers of every description— often with masses of stately lilies, some specimens of which measured six inches across, or with waving sheets of purple irises and columbines. Then gliding noiselessly across the scene would come a raft drifting

c

quietly down the river, and sadly tempting us to do the same, instead of laboriously plodding our way through the forest up the stream.

But we were now approaching the Ever-White Mountain, and the interest of attaining our goal would, we felt, repay all our exertions. As we neared it, however, our difficulties gradually increased. At Mao-erh-shan, on the Yalu, two hundred and eighty miles from Mukden, where we had expected to get all ordinary supplies, we found practically nothing. For a day or two before reaching this place, we had been living upon very short rations, and had been looking forward to eating a good square meal of meat on our arrival. But only some uneatable pork was to be had, and we were obliged to content ourselves, in the way of meat, with an egg curry, made of salted eggs six months old, and only eatable at all with the aid of a very strong flavouring by way of disguise.

We here had to leave the valley of the Yalu and plunge into the heart of the forest. Day after day we ascended the ridges which run down from the great mountain—up one side

of the ridge and down the other, then up
again, and so on everlastingly. Even from
the summits of the ridges nothing was to be
seen ; we were simply swamped in forest, and
could not see a yard beyond it. I know of
nothing more depressing than this, to struggle
on, forcing a way for the mules through the
undergrowth, hauling and shoving them up the
slopes and rocky gullies, and then tired and
exhausted and out of temper to arrive at the
top and find ourselves still hedged in by trunks
of trees, still unable to see what lay beyond.
We were, too, afflicted by a pestering scourge
of mosquitoes and midges. In the daytime we
had the midges driving us wild with their
irritating pricks, and at night the mosquitoes in
clouds descended on us. By simply closing
the hand a dozen of them could be caught at
any time. Of course we had to wear veils the
whole day long, and keep our hands in our
pockets or wrapped round with cloth ; but even
then we suffered badly, washing was a positive
torture, and we had to dash through our
ablutions and get ourselves under cover again
as rapidly as possible. Gad-flies were another
form of torture invented for these parts. They

would attack even us pretty constantly, but it was chiefly to the poor animals that they directed their attention, and the wretched mules were often covered with blood and driven wild by their attacks. Such were the conditions of travel in the deep recesses of the Manchurian forests.

At night we would put up in the sable-hunters' huts, met with every twelve or fifteen miles, each the head-quarters of a party of hunters who trap sables and also seek the ginseng root, a plant upon which the Chinese set great store for medicinal purposes. Such huts were suitable enough for the small parties who ordinarily inhabited them, but when our large party came in addition they were crammed to bursting. Yet we had to sleep in them, for to sleep outside amongst the swarms of mosquitoes and in the damp of the forest was an impossibility. We therefore packed ourselves into the huts, and were sometimes so tightly squeezed in the row on the kang, that we had to lie heads and tails with the Chinamen, to fit ourselves in at all. We had also to keep a fire burning to raise smoke for the purpose of driving off the mosquitoes ; so the heat on a summer's night and the state of the atmosphere inside may be imagined! We, of course, obtained no adequate rest, and that period of our journey was irritating and dull.

Travelling on through the forest, we reached one of the branches of the great Sungari river —an affluent of the Amur, and, at its junction, of even greater volume than that river. This stream we now ascended, as it was said to flow down from the Ever-White Mountain of which we were in search; but after two days' travelling our mules were brought to a standstill by a bog through which it was impossible to take any animal. One man for carrying loads was all we could secure, and so we had to reduce our baggage to its minimum, and each one carry his own, while the one porter carried such supplies as we should be unable to obtain ahead; for though we heard of there being one or two sable-hunters' huts, the owners of these were said to be themselves almost starving for want of food. Shouldering our loads therefore, we pushed our way through the incessant bogs which now filled up the valley, and at night put up in the huts. This was the hardest piece of work we had done, for we covered from fifteen to twenty miles a day, and that through ground where we frequently sank up to our knees in the morasses and never felt sure of our footing, while the loads which we carried made the travelling still more wearisome. Added to this was the further trial that we had to place ourselves on half-rations. Ever since entering the forest we had found difficulty in obtaining supplies; flour was very scarce, so that we had to live principally upon millet porridge, and meat was not forthcoming as often as we should have liked after our hard work. But now, as we approached the mountain and as the physical strain became greater, supplies became scarcer still, and after we had left the mules, and consequently while we were doing our hardest work, we were on fare which made me at least so ravenous that I more than once went round to the hunters' cooking-pot and scraped out all I could from the inside after they had finished their meal. On three separate occasions I remember James, Fulford, and myself all sitting down to dine off one partridge between us; this, with a little unpalatable soup and a scone, was all we had.

We had, however, the satisfaction of knowing

that we now really were approaching the great
White Mountain, the mysterious goal of our
enterprise. As we climbed higher the forest
began to open out, and on the fourth day after
leaving the mules we at last found ourselves at
its base, and saw its serried outline rising high
above the forest. It was with a sigh of infinite
relief that we looked upon it, but I cannot say
that, here in its solid reality, it inspired us with
awe commensurate with the mystery which had
been attached to it. Rising high above the
surrounding forest-clad hills, it might in the
British Isles pass muster as a mountain, but
was far from being the snow-clad monarch we
had expected to see; it afterwards proved to
be but eight thousand feet in height. Still,
here the mountain was, and what it lacked in
grandeur was made up for in beauty, for its
sides were covered with the most exquisite
meadows and copses. In Kashmir beautiful
grassy slopes are found, but none to compare
with these, the equal of which I, at least, have
never seen. Masses of colour, flowers of every
kind, whole meadows of irises, tiger-lilies and
columbines, and graceful, stately fir trees
scattered about to relieve any excess of colour

and add to the beauty of the whole. And, looking closer, we found ferns of the most delicate tracery, deep blue gentians, golden buttercups, azaleas, orchids, and numbers of other flowers of every type of beauty, all in their freshest summer bloom.

The following day we visited some springs which form one of the sources of the Sungari, and on the next we ascended the mountain itself. The trees became fewer and fewer, and we emerged on to open slopes covered with long grass and dwarf azaleas, heather, yellow poppies, and gentians. Except the steepness there was no difficulty in the ascent, and we made for a saddle between two rugged peaks which crowned the mountain. We pressed eagerly on to reach this point, as from it we hoped to look out beyond, far away over Corea on the opposite side. At last we reached the saddle, and then, instead of the long succession of alternate hills and valleys we had made up our minds we should see unfolded before us, we looked down in astonishment on a beautiful lake in a setting of weird, fantastic cliffs lying directly at our feet.

We were, in fact, on an extinct volcano.

The waters were of a deep clear blue, ever
changing in intensity of colour, and situated
here at the very summit of a mountain, and
held in on every side by frowning precipices,
this lake was unique in character as well as
position. We tried to descend to its brim,
but could find no way down the cliffs; so,
after boiling a thermometer to ascertain the
altitude, I set out to ascend the highest of the
rocky peaks which formed a fringe around it.
The climb was a stiff one, and the risk of
crashing down with one of the rocks into the
deep lake almost directly beneath me not
always remote; but at length each successive
rocky obstacle had been negotiated, and I
succeeded in reaching the summit—the very
top of the Ever-White Mountain—and from
there looked out over a billowy expanse of
forest-clad hills stretching away on every side,
as far as the eye could reach; on the one side
over Manchuria, and on the other over Corea;
nothing but forest, except where the lake below
me lay like a sapphire in a setting of rock, and
it was only by this and by occasional glints
of the river that the vast expanse of green was
broken.

But the lake was the saving feature. It appeared to be about six or seven miles in circumference, and at its farther end was an outlet, from which flowed the main branch of the Sungari. This, then, was the source of that noble river which, a few hundred miles lower down, we afterwards found to be over a mile broad, and which has claims, indeed, to be considered the main branch of the great Amur—a river excelled in size and grandeur by few others in the world.

I rejoined my companions, and we set off rapidly down the mountain-side, delighted at having successfully achieved the object of our journey, and with the feeling that all our toil had not been in vain. The Ever-White Mountain was not white with snow, and therefore not as lofty as we had been led to expect; it was white, or partially white, with pumice-stone from the old volcano. But it was a satisfaction to have established this fact, and the beauty of its flower-covered slopes and of the meadows at its base, and the impressive solitude of the wonderful lake at its summit, were ample compensation for our disappointment at its height.

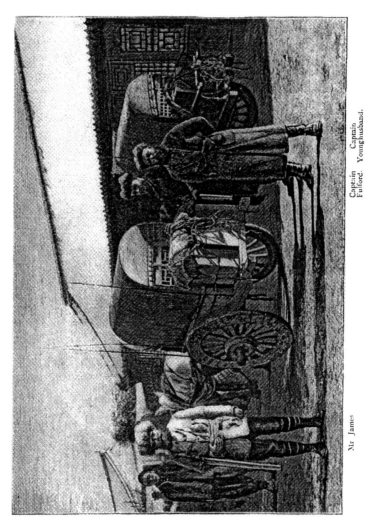

Mr James

Captain
Fulford.

Captain
Younghusband.

OUR PARTY IN MANCHURIA.

Page 22.

Three days later we were back at the place where we had left our mules, and we ravenously devoured some eggs which we managed to secure there. It is said to be good to rise from a meal with an appetite. In those days we always rose from our meals with magnificent appetites. To have no longer to carry a load was unspeakable relief, and, happiness being merely a relative quality, we felt thoroughly content on the following day as we trudged along beside the mules, with no weight on our backs to crush the spirit out of us.

Our intention now was to descend the Sungari to Kirin, one of the principal towns of Manchuria, and situated about three hundred miles from the source of the river, near where it enters the more open part of the country. We had still many days of weary plodding through the forest, climbing ridge after ridge, crossing and recrossing tributary streams, one of which we had to ford twenty-four times in the course of a single march, and everywhere waist-deep. But at length, and very suddenly, we found ourselves clear of the forest, and in a populous district of extraordinary fertility. The soil—all reclaimed from the forest—was almost black, and, judging from the crops, must have been of surpassing richness. The houses were all new, large, and well built, and provisions could be obtained in plenty. After rough travelling in uninhabited parts, one really appreciates being amongst men again, and seeing active life all round : and here, as before, we were impressed by the vigour and prosperity of these Chinese colonists breaking through the forest. In Asia one sees plenty of the old age-worn life, but on that continent it is in but few places that one can see the fresh young life of a colony pushing vigorously ahead.

On August 12 we reached Kirin, and the first round of our journey was completed. Kirin is a town of from eighty to one hundred thousand inhabitants, picturesquely situated among wooded hills, on a bend of the Sungari, here, only three hundred miles from its source, a majestic stream a quarter of a mile broad and twenty feet deep. But it rained incessantly while we were there, and the filth and smells of the place, increased in consequence, prevented us from enjoying as we should have done all its natural beauties.

The chief attraction was an arsenal recently set up here entirely by Chinamen, and managed by them alone, without any European guidance or supervision whatever.   Here we found magazine rifles, gatling guns, and field-guns being turned out in creditable fashion.   We called on the manager, who himself conducted us round the workshops.   It was he who had started the place, and we were fairly astonished to find such a really creditable establishment in the heart of Manchuria, many hundreds of miles from the coast, and in a country where there were neither railways nor waterways, nor even good roads for the carriage of the heavy and delicate machinery.   Mr. Sung, the manager, was very civil to us, and invited us to dinner, where we met some other officials of the place.   Chinese dinners are generally elaborate, and this one was no exception. Course after course was served up, till we must have had between thirty and forty, including such delicacies as sea-slugs, sharks' fins, and bird's-nest soup.   The Chinese are remarkably good cooks, and, though the dishes are often served in a way which is not palatable to Europeans, the actual cooking is excellent

There were, for instance, little suet dumplings,
so light that they almost melted in the mouth
like jelly.   Some of the dishes of vegetables
were also extremely good, and I especially recall
a plate of stewed young celery.   I cannot say,
however, that I can bestow much praise on his
liquor department.   Warmed spirit distilled
from rice is not good, and taken as incessantly
as a Chinese host expects his guest to take it,
is apt to make one decidedly heavy, if not
more.

But the point in which the Chinese most
excel in these social gatherings is in their
duty as hosts.   They are perfect hosts, full
of attention to their guests, of cheery *bonhomie*,
and of lively conversation.   There is elaborate
politeness, and a strict etiquette is observed,
but no stiffness is apparent ; every one is
cheery, and everyone talks with animation.
It was a revelation, indeed, to us to find what
good fellows these Chinamen could be amongst
themselves.   Seeing only the lower classes, the
mule-men, the loafers of the streets, and the
frequenters of the inns, one is apt to form a most
unfavourable impression of the Chinese, and to
regard them as a rude, coarse, unmannerly

race, who hate strangers, and take little trouble
to disguise their feelings.   But when one can
see Chinese gentlemen at home, one modifies
this first impression very considerably; and
personally, from this and other occasions on
which I afterwards had opportunities of meeting
Chinese gentlemen, I saw much to admire and
even to like in them.

I liked their never-failing politeness to one
another, which seemed to me too incessant
and sustained to be mere veneer, and to
indicate a real feeling of regard for one
another.   Then, again, their cheeriness is a
trait which one likes.   The general impression among Europeans is that Chinamen are
cold, hard creatures who have not a laugh in
them.   As a matter of fact, they have plenty
of heartiness and joviality when they care to
indulge in it.   I should say, too, that their
conversation is good; it is certainly bright, and
it is natural and well sustained.   In conversation
with Europeans they do not excel; they are
lamentably ignorant of geography, for instance,
and they often annoy the stranger by asking
if his country is tributary to China.   But in the
conversation carried on amongst themselves

there seem to be many topics quite as good as geography and the weather, and one hears long, well-thought-out, and well-expressed arguments on philosophic and moral subjects, freely interspersed with quotations from their classics. The philosophising Chinaman is perhaps rather too celestial, rather too much above ordinary mortals, and certainly shows too little interest in the common everyday affairs of this world : but he is an interesting man to meet at home, and, mingled with the irritation which his superciliousness so often inspires, I had a feeling of real regard for a man who can aspire to such a lofty standpoint as the Chinaman looks to, and in his case I felt that the seeming superciliousness was not all simple self-conceit, but that he had in him the pride engendered by belonging to an empire which has stood intact for thousands of years, and which was approaching civilisation when we ourselves were steeped in barbarism.

CHAPTER II.

NORTHERN MANCHURIA.

On September 3, after a three weeks' rest, we
set out once more on our travels, heading this
time towards Tsi-tsi-har. The roads were to
be comparatively level and good, so we were
able to return to the use of carts, and travel
over twenty-five miles or more daily. But the
season was bad, rain had been falling constantly,
and in consequence the roads—of course none
of them metalled—were simply quagmires.
Even just outside Kirin we stuck hopelessly
for a couple of hours in a mass of mud, and
delays more or less lengthy were constant.
But we had three mules to each cart, and
when one cart was badly stuck we harnessed
on a team from another to help, and in this
way managed to get over more ground each
day than the state of the roads would have led
one to believe possible. The hills became

lower and lower and the valleys wider as we
proceeded, till we soon found ourselves in open
undulating country, very richly cultivated and
thickly inhabited. The crops, now in full ear,
were extraordinarily heavy; the millet especially, both the large and the small, being unusually heavy in the ear. The villages, too, were
all of considerable size and numerous. But
separate farmhouses or small hamlets were
seldom seen—probably on account of the
brigandage, which was very rife all over
North Manchuria. We heard frequent tales
of carts being attacked on the road, and of
villages and even towns being pillaged. We
had, however, no personal experience of these
·brigands, and this part of our journey, though
interesting as lying through a populous and
thriving district, was lacking in incident and
excitement.

Just beyond Petuna we again struck the
Sungari, here spread out in many channels to a
width of some ten miles. We crossed it by
a ferry, and on the opposite side we soon
entered the open rolling steppes of Mongolia.
The rich cultivation ceased, and with it the
villages, so that we now only passed an occa-

sional hut inhabited by Mongols, and entered
on a quite new phase of our journey. Scarcely
a tree was to be seen, and for mile after mile
we passed over rolling downs covered with rich
grass and exquisite flowers.* In the hollows
were often lakes of considerable size, some of
them several miles in length. And these were
covered with swarms of water-fowl—thousands
and thousands of duck and geese. Indeed,
these lakes must have been the breeding-ground
of the water-fowl, which, in the cold weather,
find their way down to the warmer parts of the
continent. Large numbers of bustard, too, we
saw, and many herds of antelope.

The chief attraction for us, however, at this
period of our journey, was the milk and cream
we could obtain. What a treat, indeed, it was,
after nearly four months without milk or any
of its products, to drink some of the rich
delicious stuff which these Mongols brought
us! At one time in the forest, when I had
been out of sorts, I had been allowed a glass
of condensed milk from our stores as a medical

* The whole of this tract from Petuna to Tsi-tsi-har is
now under cultivation, so rapid has been the advance of
Chinese colonisation.

D 2

comfort; to get even this was such a luxury
that I was sorely tempted to feign sickness
for another day to obtain more! But here
was the pure article in any quantity, and as
rich and thick with cream as any from Devon-
shire.

Of the Mongols we saw very little. They
were probably removed from the main line of
traffic, to keep well clear of the shady characters
who might frequent it. We only came across
two of the felt yurts which are their characteristic abodes, and those Mongols whom we did
meet lived in houses, and were more or less
tamed and settled.

At length, on September 20, we reached
Tsi-tsi-har, a large town of about forty or fifty
thousand inhabitants, and the seat of government of the province of the same name, which
fills up the whole of North Manchuria. But
there was little to see beyond the ordinary
shops, the dirty streets, and tumble-down
temples of any Chinese town. This was the
most northern point we reached. Winter was
approaching, and already we had felt some
touches of frost. We had yet much ground to
get over, and so we struck off back again

towards the Sungari, making this time for Hulan about two hundred miles distant.

This we found to be a new and thriving town only recently built, and surrounded with a strong masonry wall. The shops were excellent, and there was a busy, bustling air about the whole place. But it had in the previous year been attacked by a band of brigands, who had sought out the principal merchants, levied black-mail from them, and then decamped. It was here, too, that a French missionary, Père Conraux, had been most cruelly tortured and almost killed in the year previous to our visit.

From this point we turned to Pa-yen-su-su, a Roman Catholic mission station, where we found both its own director and M. Card from Pei-lin-tzŭ. It was indeed a pleasure to see these men, and to have that warm, heartfelt greeting which one European will give to another, of whatever nationality, in the most distant corners of the world. Except the French consul who had been sent to inquire into the outrage on Père Conraux in the previous year, no European had ever before visited these distant mission stations, and we,

on our part, had not met a European for
several months now, so the delight of this
meeting may be well imagined. But, apart
from that, we were very deeply impressed by
the men themselves. Few men, indeed, have
ever made a deeper impression on me than did
these simple missionaries. They were standing,
transparent types of all that is best in man.
They seemed to diffuse an atmosphere of pure
genuine goodness which made itself felt at
once. And we recognised immediately that
we were not only with *good* but with *real* men.
What they possessed was no weak sentimen-
tality or flashy enthusiasm, but solid human
worth. Far away from their friends, from all
civilisation, they lived, and worked, and died ;
two, indeed, out of the three we met in those
parts, have died since we left. When they left
France, they left it for good ; they had no
hope of return ; they went out for their whole
lives.

These missionaries may not make many
converts, but they do good. No man, Chinaman or European, who came in contact for
five minutes with M. Raguit, M. Card, or
M. Riffard, whom we afterwards met, could

help feeling the better for it. Their strong yet
gentle and simple natures, developed by the
hardships of their surroundings and the loftiness
of their ideals, and untainted by the contact
with worldly praise and glamour, impressed
itself on us at once, and, as we saw evidenced
in the people around, had affected the Chinese
likewise.

> "Great deeds cannot die;
> They, with the sun and moon, renew their light
> For ever, blessing those that look on them."

Others may bring discredit on the missionary
cause, and produce the feeling of hostility to it
which undoubtedly exists, but these are the
men who are a true light in the world, and
who will spread abroad the essence of Chris-
tianity—the doing of good to others.

This remote mission station—established here
where no other Europeans had penetrated—
was a source of the greatest interest to us, and
fulfilled our highest ideal of such a station.
There was here no elaborate costly house, no
air of luxury, such as may be seen in many
missionary establishments elsewhere, but everything was of the most rigorous simplicity.
There was merely a plain little house, almost

bare inside, and with stiff, simple furniture.
Under such hard conditions, with such plain
surroundings, and shut off for ever from inter-
course with the civilised world, it might be
supposed that these missionaries would be dull,
stern, perhaps morbid men. But they were
precisely the contrary. They had a fund of
simple joviality, and were hearty and full of
spirits. They spoke now and then with a sigh
of "la belle France," but they were evidently
thoroughly happy in their lives, and devoted to
their work.

From these simple hospitable mission stations
we made our way to Sansing. Every day now
the weather was becoming colder, and at one
place we were delayed for a day by a very
heavy snowstorm. We had to hurry along,
for the missionaries had assured us that in
winter the thermometer fell to over 40° below
zero Fahrenheit, and had showed us a thermometer which they had used, on which they had
seen the mercury fall to $-47°$ Centigrade. The
country we passed through was now hilly, and
covered with copses of wood—oak and birch.
We might have been passing through an
English county; and on the edges of these

copses we regularly found some excellent pheasant-shooting. All day long, too, flock after flock of geese flew by us overhead, making towards the south. Usually these were a long way out of shot, but on a windy day they would often be forced down so as just to top the hills, and then from the summit we would get a shot at them as they flew over.

We once more crossed the Sungari, and on October 13 reached Sansing, an older town than those we had recently passed through, and with much less life and bustle about it. Very good furs, however, were to be obtained here, and, as hard winter might be on us any day now, we fitted ourselves out with long loose sheepskin coats, reaching well down to the ankles. Sansing is the farthest inhabited place of any importance in the direction of the Amur. The Sungari is here quite navigable for boats of considerable size, and consequently the Chinese had erected near by some fortifications of considerable strength. We rode out to see them, and I was astonished to find a fort constructed of earthwork, and planned on the most approved European lines, and armed with Krupp guns of six or seven tons' weight.

After a couple of days' rest at Sansing, we
turned southward and ascended the Hurka
river to Ninguta.   The road was execrable.
We still had our carts, and how we, or rather
the drivers, managed to get them along a road
really fit only for pack-animals was a marvel.
There was a constant series of ascents and
descents of spurs running down to the river.
These were nearly always steep, and the road
narrow and rocky.   Small villages were only
occasionally met with, and the country was far
less well populated than that we had recently
come through.   The hills were covered with
woods of oak and birch, and their summits with
pines.   Amongst them, it was said, there were
gold-mines, which, however, it was only per-
missible for government to work, as the
Chinese think that indiscriminate gold-mining
only leads to fighting, quarrelling and trouble ;
the emperor therefore absolutely forbids his
subjects to mine for gold.   We crossed
numerous side streams, and these, as well
as the Hurka itself, swarm with fish, mostly
salmon.   The natives form dams across the
side streams, and catch them in hundreds.   So
at this time, what with pheasants, ducks, geese,

and salmon, we were living luxuriously enough to make up for our privations in the forests of the White Mountain.

As we neared Ninguta the valley opened up into a wide plain, which was well cultivated and populated, and on October 26 we reached Ninguta, a flourishing place of nearly twenty thousand inhabitants. Here we found a telegraph station just opened. The Chinese attach considerable importance to this frontier, touching as it does on Russian territory, and the construction of this telegraph line was one of the signs of the interest they took in it. The line was well and stoutly constructed under the supervision of a Danish gentleman. But the office was manned entirely by Chinese, and the language in use was English. Every clerk spoke English, and it was a pleasure to us to meet any one who spoke our native tongue.

We halted here a couple of days, and then started for Hunchun, a garrison post of some importance, situated on the extreme frontier, and just at the point where Russian, Chinese, and Corean territory meet. Winter was creeping on apace now. The thermometer

on the morning we left Ninguta was at
11° Fahrenheit, so we had to push on hard
to get to our farthest destination, which we
hoped might be on the sea, at the Russian port
just beyond Hunchun, and then back to our
original starting-point at Newchwang, before
the severest part of the Manchurian winter
overtook us. The road was terribly bad, again
crossing over ridges fifteen hundred to two
thousand feet in height, passing over heavy
bogs and morasses, and through forests of pine,
birch, and oak.

Hunchun we found to be simply a garrison
town. There were here about three thousand
troops, and the small town there served for
little else than to supply their wants. But we
discovered in it a number of European articles
which had been imported from the Russian
station close by. Clocks, sweets, soap, canned
fruits, and many other luxuries were to be
obtained here, and at a very reasonable price.
We bought a can of Singapore pineapples for
a shilling. In the direction of the Russian
frontier, which was only ten miles distant, were
some strong forts mounted with heavy Krupp
guns.

From Hunchun Mr. James had written to
the commander of the Russian post across the
frontier, saying that we were unprovided with
passports to travel in Russian territory ; but
that, if he would give us permission to do so,
we should like to visit Novo-kievsk. We then
started off towards Russian territory. Just as
we reached the frontier, we descried a couple of
horsemen trotting towards us, and as they drew
near, we saw that they were unmistakably
Cossacks. Neither of us had seen a mounted
Cossack before ; but their resemblance to all
the pictures one sees of them in illustrated
papers and books was evidence enough who
they were.   There was the same rough,
shaggy-looking grey sheepskin cap, long over-
coats, high boots, whip, and rifle slung over the
back, that we knew so well from pictures.
They saluted, and gave Mr. James a letter
from Colonel Sokolowski, who commanded the
Russian post. The colonel said he would be
most happy to allow us to cross the frontier,
and that he hoped that we would visit his post
and "accept the cordial but frugal hospitality
of a Cossack." We rode on, therefore, and at
about three miles from the frontier came across

the Russian station of Swanka, situated among some low rather bare hills. There were stationed here at the time of our visit about three hundred Cossacks. Some low rough barracks had just been constructed for them, and small cottages for the officers were dotted about. The colonel's house was larger and better built, but all of them were of the rough simple description one would expect to find at a distant frontier outpost.

Here we were most cordially received by the Russian colonel. Russians never err in want of cordiality—to Englishmen especially—and in this remotest part of Asia, thousands of miles from either St. Petersburg or London, we met, uninvited guests as we were, with real warmth of reception. The colonel's house had about it no superfluity of luxury. It had glass windows and a stove—which are luxuries the Russian would not have met with if he had visited my late headquarters in Chitral—but the walls and the floors were quite bare, and the furniture of the very simplest. There was only one room, a part of which was partitioned off into a bedroom and dressing-room, and the whole place was crowded up with military

stores—for a Russian colonel seems to be his
own quarter-master and storekeeper—and all
about the room were piles of saddlery, racks of
arms, and heaps of miscellaneous articles of
Cossack equipment.

We had some light refreshment, and then
the colonel took us round to see the barracks.
Here the Cossacks were still hard at work,
completing the building before winter set in.
They were hard, strong-looking men, fair in
complexion, with cheery good-natured faces;
and there was about them a workmanlike air,
which gave one the idea that they could and
would turn their hands to anything. An
English soldier is perfectly right when he has
shaken down on active service, but in barracks
he produces the impression that his dress is his
main interest in life. A Cossack, on the other
hand, wherever one meets him, looks as if he
were ready to buckle to and fight there and
then; and certainly dress or appearance is the
last thing in the world he would trouble his
head about. The barracks they had just constructed were rough but clean, and about as
good as those of our native troops in India.
They were inferior to those of the Chinese

troops over the way at Hunchun, but they were evidently of a temporary description. The rations of the Cossacks consisted principally of black bread, and they received also an allowance of soup-like stew or stew-like soup; but the whole ration was decidedly inferior to what the British soldier gets. Their pay is twenty roubles—about fifty shillings—a month, which would be very liberal if they had not out of it to pay for the whole of their equipment. The amount which actually reaches their pocket was, according to the colonel, about a halfpenny a day! It must indeed require conscription to induce men to go through all a Cossack does for this ludicrous remuneration.

In the evening the colonel had a small dinner-party, when three of the officers of the post and a Chinaman, who spoke Russian, and acted as interpreter between the Russian and Chinese officials, came in. After eating some small dishes, such as sardines and salmon chips, at a side table, and washing them down with a glass or two of vodka, which the colonel informed us was a quite necessary proceeding, to clear our throats for the dinner that was

coming, we sat down to the main business.
First of all, a great soup-tureen was placed on
the table, filled with a good substantial soup.
"No ceremony, gentlemen; *je mange énorme-
ment*," said the colonel.   And he proceeded to
ladle himself out a good helping, and every one
round the table then did the same.   Each of us
had at his side six bottles of wine and beer,
and these we were expected to attack indis-
criminately.   "You're drinking nothing," shouts
out the colonel, as he stretches across the table
and fills my glass with claret.   Before that was
finished, another officer would fill my glass—
the same glass!—with sherry.   Then the
colonel would insist upon our trying the beer.
Meanwhile course after course of the most
substantial dishes were being served up.   Each
one helped himself from them, but in addition
one or other of the officers would cut off a huge
slice and put it down in one of our plates.   The
hospitality was genuine and most hearty; but
how we got through that evening was a marvel
to us.   We had been leading a hard, healthy
life lately, so had good appetites, and were able
to keep fairly well in line with the Russians in
the eating way.   But the drinking was terrible.

E

If we had been allowed to keep at one liquor we might possibly have survived; but the mixture of port and beer, and sherry and claret, and Guinness's stout and vodka, backwards and forwards, first one and then the other, was fatal!

After we had eaten and drunk and talked for some hours, the other officers went off, and the colonel said to us, " I don't know quite where you will sleep.   There is a sofa for one of you ; the other two had better sleep on the floor." This we proceeded to do, and so passed our first night in Russian territory.   The colonel had spoken of his Cossack hospitality being rough but cordial.   It was both.

On the following day we started for the larger station of Novo-kievsk, fifteen miles distant, and situated on the coast.   It turned out to be but a small place with a garrison of a battalion of infantry, a battery of artillery, and about a hundred mounted Cossacks.   There were very few buildings besides the barracks. The roadways were unmetalled, and the whole place had a dreary, uncared-for appearance. We could discover no Russian hotel or inn of any description, and had to put up at a

Chinese inn. The whole place, barracks, shops, church, and everything, was not so large, and certainly not so well built, as the barracks of my regiment in India.

We were close here to the Corean frontier, so there were numbers of Coreans about. Many are settled in this valley, and seem to flourish, and to be looked upon with favour by the Russian authorities. They appeared to me to be rather a dull, insipid race, but they are said to be quiet and orderly, and as the Russians want population to cultivate and improve the land, so much of which is now merely run to waste, they are welcomed to Russian territory to carry out the work of which the Russians themselves seem incapable. Colonel Sokolowski told us that his government were extremely anxious to have all this Eastern Siberia colonised by Russians. They gave every encouragement they could to settlers; free farming implements, horses, and cattle, and brought them out from Russia free of expense; but the settlers had no energy or vigour; they accepted all that was given them, and set to work to produce enough to live on, but nothing beyond. "If you English," said the colonel, "had had this country, you would have made a magnificent place of it by now ; but our Russians have none of that colonising spirit you have, and the country is only slowly opened up."   Since that time, however, the Siberian railway has been taken in hand.   The Russians are waking up in earnest, and a great future ought to lie before these magnificently fertile tracts of Eastern Siberia.   What the Chinese colonists have been able to do on their side of the border is a type of what the Russians could do also.   And with a railway to aid in its development, all these regions about the Amur and its tributaries ought to equal the most thriving parts of Canada.

CHAPTER III.

BACK TO PEKING.

WE now turned our faces homewards. We had
reached the limit of our journey, and now had
to hurry back to the coast at Newchwang.
Mr. James went by a short cut to Kirin, while
Fulford and I, with the carts, travelled round
by Ninguta to meet a man whom we expected
with letters. On November 11 we left Hunchun, and now winter had regularly set in.
The thermometer was at zero or a degree or
two above or below it, and snow was beginning
to fall. At Ninguta we found the river, which
we had three weeks before crossed in a ferry,
and which was about one hundred and fifty
yards broad and with a by no means slow
current, now frozen over so completely that
we could run our heavily laden carts over on
the ice. Here we at last received letters, the
first batch since we had started on our journey

six months before, and, after all the hardships and the frequent *ennui* of travel, the delight of getting in touch again with one's friends and inhaling one soft breath of air from our native land was intense and almost bewildering. It made us forget all the hard part we had gone through; that all seemed a dream now, and just that touch from outside put enough new energy into us to have started us contentedly on another fresh journey if need had been.

Fulford and I met with no incident on our road to Kirin, though we passed the body of a man who had on the previous day been murdered by brigands; and on November 26 we rejoined Mr. James at Kirin. The great Sungari was now frozen over hard. The ice on it was more than a foot thick, and we were able to trot our carts smoothly across a river three hundred yards wide and twenty feet deep.

From Kirin we pushed on rapidly to Mukden. The cold was now becoming intense. On account of the heavy traffic on the road, we had to make early starts in the morning so as to secure places at the inns in the evening. We rose at two or three, had a good plate of porridge and some tea, and then started off. For the first hour or two it would, of course, be dark. Snow covered the ground, and the thermometer would read anything from zero to 14° Fahrenheit below zero, which was the coldest we registered. But though it was so cold, I do not remember suffering from it. The air was generally still, and we had the advantage of starting from a warm house with something warm inside us, and at the end of our day's march, we again found a good warm room to go to. It was afterwards, on the Pamirs and in the Himalayas, that I really felt the cold, for there, instead of a warm room to start from, I only had a small tent, and sometimes no tent at all, nor sufficient firewood for a fire, and the high altitudes, by causing breathlessness and bringing on weakness, added to my discomfort. Here in Manchuria, unless it happened to be windy—and then, of course, it was really trying—the cold affected us but little. The roads were frozen hard and the snow on them well beaten down by the heavy traffic, and we trundled along a good thirty miles a day.

The traffic in this winter season was immense. I counted in a single day's march over eight hundred carts, all heavily laden and drawn by teams of at least two and many of them nine animals, ponies or mules. A main road in Manchuria in the winter is a busy scene, and these strings of carts rolling along on the frosty morning, with the jingling bells of the teams, and the drivers shouting at their animals, were signs of animation which we had hardly expected to see after our first experience on the heavy, muddy roads in the summer. The inns were numerous and crowded, and as a string of carts passed by each, men would come running out, proclaiming the advantages of their particular hostelry, and trying to persuade the carters to come in. Then, when the carts stopped, the inn men would bustle about, fetching grain and fodder for the animals and food for the men, and there was as much life and activity as in a country town in England on market day. I remarked, too, how very well the carters fed their animals. These Manchurian, or rather Mongolian, ponies and mules are never allowed blankets or clothing of any description, and stand out quite bare all

COURTYARD OF A CHINESE INN.

Page 56.

night in a cold so great that I have even seen the hoar frost lying thick on an animal's back in the morning. But they are fed enormously while they are in work. They are given in the day as much as sixteen pounds of grain, besides bran and chopped millet-stalks. When they are not at work they are eating, and the eating and the work together occupy so much time that I could never discover when they slept!

The country we passed through was pretty even in winter, and must have been really beautiful in summer. It was undulating, well covered with trees, and intersected with many little streams and rivers. At this season all was under snow, but one morning we saw one of the most perfectly lovely sights I have ever seen—a *frozen* mist. As the sun rose we found the whole air glittering with brilliant particles sparkling in the rays of the sun—and the mist had encrusted everything, all the trunks of the trees and all the delicate tracery of their out-lines, with a coating like hoar frost. The earth, the trees, and everything around was glistening white, and the whole air sparkling in the sunlight. It lasted but a short while, for as the sun rose the mist melted away, but for the time one seemed to be verily in a fairyland.

We passed through many villages and thriving little towns, and at length, after covering the last ninety miles in two days, we arrived at Mukden and found ourselves among our own countrymen again.　We drove up to the Scottish mission established here, the members of which had been particularly kind to us on our previous visit to Mukden, and had pressed us to stay with them on our return.　Messrs. Ross and Webster and Dr. Christie came running out of the house as they saw us driving up in the cart, and it was only as we were shown into a cosy drawing-room, where the ladies were having tea, that we realised how rough we had grown on the journey.　We had each of us developed a beard, which, as well as our hair, now, in the light of civilisation, seemed most unkempt.　Our faces were burning red from the exposure, and our clothes—especially our boots—were worn out and torn with the rough wear they had undergone.　We had had many trials on the journey, but this facing a ladies' tea-party in a drawing-room in our disreputable condition was the hardest of them all !

This Scottish mission is established with a special object, and on lines different from most other missions. The object is to try and get at the Chinese officials and gentry; to preach to the lower class as well, but to make an especial attempt to get in touch with the gentry and upper classes of society. With this object, highly trained men are sent out, and the mission is established with some "style," though I use this word not to imply any particularly luxurious surroundings, but rather to impress the difference from the extremely simple and plain establishment of other missions which I have seen. It is recognised that Chinese officials are reluctant to mix freely with men who live in very humble houses and dress indifferently, and it is thought that men who adopt a higher style of living and dress will have more chance of meeting with these sensitive Chinamen. It is, moreover, considered by the heads of this mission that men will work better in a distant land if they are accompanied by their wives to cheer and encourage them and help on the mission work by teaching children. It is part, too, of the general line of action that at each mission station there should also be a missionary doctor, through whom first access may be gained to men who might otherwise never be approachable.

This class of mission does not inspire the same amount of enthusiasm, as, for instance, that of the French missionaries we had met in Northern Manchuria; but it may be quite as effective, and for the immediate object, that of gaining access to the higher classes, it is probably much better suited. The medical part of the mission, especially, is eminently practical, and likely to be appreciated by the people. As we ourselves saw, high Chinese officials did make use of the services of Dr. Christie, and, though it cannot be expected that, because a man is cured of an illness, he should straightway become a Christian, it is evidently an advantage to both the Chinaman and the missionary that they should have had the opportunity of coming in contact with one another. Something of the strong earnest character of the medical missionary must be reflected on to the Chinaman, and the missionary on his side will have been able to learn something of the prejudices and difficulties of the educated classes of the Chinese.

We could only spare one full day's halt at Mukden, and we then pushed on to New-chwang, where we arrived on December 19, just seven months after we had left it.

At Newchwang our party broke up; Mr. James went off to Port Arthur and thence to Japan, while Mr. Fulford and I proceeded to Peking. After these years I feel strongly how much I owe to Mr. James. It was through him that I had thus gained my first experience of real travelling, and, though I did not appreciate it at the time, afterwards, when I had myself to head an expedition, I realised what sterling qualities of steady, dogged perseverance he must have possessed to lead our party successfully through the forests to the mysterious Ever-White Mountain. And I have never ceased to wonder that a man, who had held high offices in India and been accustomed to the luxurious style of camp life of an Indian civil officer, should in his holiday-time choose to rough it as Mr. James did. As I used to see him marching sturdily along through the forest, the marshes, and especially when he had to carry his kit on his back, I used to marvel. To a young subaltern the thing was natural, but when a high Indian official of more than twenty years' standing did it, there must have been in him a wonderful amount of "go" and pluck, and this Mr. James undoubtedly possessed.

After parting with Mr. James, Fulford and I started for Tientsin. We passed nothing of interest till we reached Shan-hai-kuan, the point where the Great Wall of China begins, or ends, in the sea. A line of hills between two or three thousand feet in height, stretched from inland close down to the seashore; and all along these heights, as far as the eye could reach, ran this wonderful wall, going down the side of one hill, up the next, over its summit and down the other side again, and then at the end finally plunging right into the sea. It was no trumpery little wall, nor such a wall, for instance, as one sees round a modern prison, but a regular castle wall, such as men built in the Middle Ages round their strongest castles, thirty or forty feet high, of solid stone, and fifteen feet or so thick, wide enough for two carriages to drive abreast on it, with towers every few hundred yards. This was the Great Wall of China at its commencement, and it is, I think, almost more wonderful than the Pyramids. I have seen both. Both astounded me by their evidence of colossal industry ; but the Great Wall of China, pushing straight over the mountains, regardless of height and distance, is, perhaps, the more impressive of the two. There are points, however, in which the Pyramids excel the Great Wall. The Pyramids are perfect throughout. Not a flaw can be found. Each huge block is laid with absolute precision, and there is no sign inside or out of anything less enduring than these immense blocks of stone being employed. Each one is an emblem of all that is rigid, exact and stable. The Great Wall, on the other hand, though it runs for hundreds of miles in the magnificent state I have described, dwindles down eventually to a mere mud wall, and, moreover, even in the best parts, the inside is only rubbish. It is not perfect throughout its entire length, nor solid right through. The Pyramids will remain when the Great Wall has run to ruin.

On New Year's Day, 1887, we reached

Tientsin, and from there I proceeded to Peking and enjoyed a welcome three months' rest, first under the hospitable roof of Mr. (now Sir Walter) Hillier and afterward with Sir John and Lady Walsham.

CHAPTER IV.

OUR INTERESTS IN MANCHURIA.

THOSE who have done me the honour of even glancing through the preceding pages, cannot fail to have been struck by evidences of the extraordinary richness of Manchuria, the salubrity of its climate, the fertility of its soil, the magnificence of its forests, and the many indications of its mineral wealth. And when the observant reader remembers also what has been said in regard to the intelligence, the industry, and the energy of the inhabitants, and hears that these number not less than twenty millions, he will be able to agree with Mr. James and me, that we acted wisely in making so promising a country the field of our explorations. The events of the twelve years which have passed since we made our journey, the pressure which the Japanese have exerted on the one side, and the Russians on the other, and the

F

first impetus to development which this pressure has given, have only served to indicate with greater clearness the importance of this valuable country.

There may then be some use in here gathering together the general results of the journey of nearly three thousand miles in the interior of Manchuria which we had now completed, and in pointing out how we as a nation are interested in so distant a land.

Though we have no need to study the climate of Manchuria with the same interest as we would have to study the climate of a country likely in the future to be settled with people of our own race, we must know some little about so important a factor in the natural development of the people. Visiting the country directly from the enervating plains of India, my companion and I were necessarily impressed with its invigorating nature. The summer heat was tempered by plentiful showers of rain, and the winter cold, though extreme, was rendered bearable by the frequent sunshine. The climate of Manchuria is indeed practically the same as that of Eastern Canada. Consequently, the inhabitants are healthy and robust, and as the rainfall is adequate and the soil unsurpassed in fertility, the crops in the cultivated plains, and the forests in more mountainous parts are magnificent. Moreover, Manchuria is spared the one great drawback to most countries in which the winter temperature falls as low as 30° or 40° below zero Fahrenheit. The snow-fall is not so heavy as to prevent traffic, and the winter season is in fact the time when the greater part of the traffic is carried on, for then the swamps are frozen, the muddy tracks of summer are converted into hard, firm roads, and carts can trundle over them as on the best macadam. And if crops are prevented from maturing for half the year they are at any rate all the fuller on that account when they do ripen. The moisture is retained in the ground, and forms a sort of reservoir to moisten the roots, while the warm sunshine of the spring and early summer acts on the upper growth.

The configuration of the country is no less favourable to development than the climate. The Russians have already cut off from Manchuria its northern coastline which includes the valuable port of Vladivostok and the important

harbour of Possiet Bay which we visited in
1886. But, on the south, there are several
hundred miles of coastline on which are situated
the Treaty Port of Newchwang, the great naval
base, Port Arthur, and the valuable harbour of
Talien-wan Bay; the two latter of which are
open all the year round. Manchuria cannot,
therefore, be called inaccessible. Foreign goods
can readily reach its doors, the country products
can be as easily exported, while immigration
from the over-crowded districts of China Proper
flows naturally to it. Its great navigable rivers
render access to the interior still more easy.
The great Amur and its tributaries, the Sungari
and the Ussuri, are navigable for hundreds of
miles, and steam launches have penetrated so
far into the interior as Kirin. In the south,
the Yalu and the Liao rivers are both navigable for some distance from their mouth,
and are most valuable for the means they offer
of floating rafts of timber down them to the
coast.

The hilly character of so great a portion of
the country is somewhat of a drawback to development, for the distant mountain glens afford
asylums for lawless brigands, and over a succes-

sion of ranges and outlying spurs it is of course
difficult to build roads and railways. The
hilly portions of Manchuria for a long time
after the plain country had become settled
were inhabited by independent tribes, and
when in years to come railways are constructed, these tracts which form unfortunately
the greater portion of the country will always
remain behind the rest. Yet it must not
be imagined that the hilly tracts of Manchuria
are comparable to those of the Indian frontier
or of the Caucasus. They are much more like
Wales, or the Highlands of Scotland. And
this drawback in the country is in part made
up for by the fertility of the valleys, and the
richness of the forests which everywhere clothe
the mountain sides. There are thousands of
square miles of the most valuable timber forest,
not only of pine but of hard woods, like oak
and elm and walnut. These forests, situated
on large rivers upon which their timber may be
easily floated to the coast, may be reckoned as
a capital of millions of pounds in the wealth of
the country, and will one day make Manchuria
famous.

But Manchuria is not all hills, and the plain

which runs from the south into the heart of the country is of sufficient extent to support twenty or thirty million people.   Here, where communication from town to town and from the interior to the sea-coast is easy, progress has always been rapid.   And the fertility of the soil is such that crops of millet, wheat, barley, beans, rice, hemp, etc., scarcely to be equalled elsewhere, are grown.   Food is, therefore, abundant and cheap, and there is ample surplus production for export.

As a result of this abundance, man and beast are well fed, and with the neighbouring pasture-lands of Mongolia to serve as a breeding ground, and with a plentiful supply of grain always at hand in the agricultural districts, the domestic animals are numerous.   The inhabitant of Manchuria need never want for sheep or cattle for slaughter, oxen or ponies for his plough, or mules and donkeys for his carts. Agricultural operations are, therefore, easily carried on, the produce is with little expense transported to market, and the means of proceeding from one district to another are readily available.   In all these respects development is greatly favoured.

If in addition to these many natural advantages, the country were also blessed with mineral wealth, etc., its future would indeed be assured, but as yet we have in this respect only indications and no certain facts. This much, however, I can say, that in several different parts we heard of gold as well as of coal, and that in one place we found gold, silver, coal and iron within a few miles of one another. That little has so far been heard of the mineral wealth of Manchuria is due to the fact that the Chinese Government absolutely prohibit mining by private individuals.

This fertile land, blessed as it is with a favourable climate, navigable rivers and capacious harbours, possesses the further all-important advantage that it is populated by an advanced and industrious race. Of the twenty million inhabitants, probably ninety-five per cent. are Chinese, and the remainder of that race which two and a half centuries ago conquered the whole of China and nominally rule it to the present day. The industry and intelligence of the Chinese are proverbial, and in Manchuria, both Mr. James and I were especially struck with the energy they showed as pioneers in a new country.   They are deficient in military aptitude and spirit, the result of which will probably be that they will have to give way before one or other of the more highly organised military powers pressing on them. Moreover, their strong conservative instincts which bind them down to methods unadapted to new requirements, and their lack of constructive imagination which indicates a merely imitative ability, should lead us to suppose that no very high form of development is likely to occur.   And their foolish superstitions often stand sadly in the way of progress.

Yet, notwithstanding these decided drawbacks, there are still sufficient grounds for prophesying a great advance in coming years. We have to regard the immensely powerful influences now being brought to bear upon the country.   We have to take into account those changes in the environing conditions which modern science has effected.   Up to the present century Manchuria was surrounded on the north by barbarous tribes.   Coreans had in ancient days made frequent invasions, but neither from across the Amur nor by sea had pressure ever been brought upon Manchuria.

Nowadays, however, the railway has brought the Russians in force on to the northern frontier, and with the completion of the Great Siberian Railway, a few years hence, in place of the weak and scattered tribes of the last century, Manchuria will find a strong civilised military power weighing down upon her. Similarly steam navigation has not only strengthened the position of Russia on the Manchurian border, by enabling her firmly to establish herself on the northern ports, which she filched away from China, at a time when she was fighting both ourselves and the French ; but it has brought military and commercial powers like Japan and Great Britain right up to the doors of Manchuria.   Distant powers, which in themselves are yearly growing more powerful, have been brought as it were into almost direct contact with the country, which is thus being compressed by a number of forces never felt before.

The result of this new pressure must inevitably be advancement and development. It may mean the effacement of the present rulers, and the substitution of rulers with more capacity for military organisation.   But in

any case the country will advance. Even at
the time of our visit, a dozen years ago,
the pressure of the Russians had caused the
Chinese to construct telegraph lines throughout
the country. The establishment of an arsenal
at Kirin, for purely military purposes, forced
them to search for coal and so open mines.
And similar military pressure from the Japanese,
as well as the Russians, is now inducing them
to extend the railways from north to south.
So that military pressure alone has resulted
in the adoption of those measures which, of all
others, most conduce to industrial development.

And there is other than merely military
pressure bearing on Manchuria. Japan, India,
America, and all the states of Europe, are by
the advance of steam navigation brought alongside, and London is to-day for practical commercial purposes scarcely more distant from
the capital of Manchuria than is Peking. Last
century not one of these countries wished to
trade with Manchuria. To-day all are clamour-
ing for access to what may not inappropriately
be called a Land of Promise. All are striving
to obtain the means by which they may intro-
duce their own manufactures to sell to the

millions of inhabitants, who must need them,
and exchange for those manufactures the raw
produce of this fertile country. What is of
still greater significance, a strong conviction is
growing up among these more advanced states,
keenly struggling for existence as they are,
that no people have the right to keep exclusively to themselves portions of the earth's
surface, the proper exploitation of which would
conduce to the general welfare of mankind.
These nations will demand with ever-increasing
insistence that the rulers of Manchuria should
not allow these vast natural riches to be unused
and run to waste. Competition for access to
parts of the world, so prolific of all that goes
to increase material prosperity and to provide
for the natural wants of a growing and wide-
spreading population, becomes more stringent
every year, and Manchuria can no longer resist
the pressure on it.

It is our business to see that Manchuria
remains as open to our trade as it now is; that
we continue in future to enjoy all the rights we
at present possess. Our first great right is that
we shall not be called upon to pay higher duties
than are required from any foreign nation.

And our second great right is that the British
Government and its subjects shall be allowed
equal participation in all the privileges which
may be granted to the Government or subjects
of any other nation.

Such are our rights, which it may be well to
remember were only acquired after years of
negotiation, and after fighting more than one
war with the Chinese; and which, it will be
noticed, are neither selfish nor exclusive. These
rights—little as they are—it is all important
that we should maintain; that we should see in
future that no impediments are placed in the
way of the investment of British capital, and
that no commercial privileges which we at
present possess should be impaired.   Manchuria is not a Turkestan nor a Uganda nor
a Rhodesia.   It is an exceedingly valuable
country, with both present wealth and future
potentialities.   The foreign trade with it is
already valued at three and a half millions
sterling, even with only one Treaty Port, and
that closed by ice for half the year, and with no
railways in the country.   Of the 664,000 tons of
shipping the British flag covers 349,600 tons,
while the Russian flag covers 3,628 tons only.

And according to Mr. Henry Norman Manchuria
is already taking more British goods than our
oldest colony, Newfoundland.   Now, with two
more ports added—Talienwan and Chang-wang-
tan—and one at least an ice free-port, with
railways constructed from end to end of the
country ; with the Chinese population so rapidly
increasing and opening out new districts ; the
trade will, if unchecked, increase with compound
acceleration.   It has indeed been calculated
that, if the rate of increase of the last ten years
be maintained during the next two decades, in
twenty years' time the foreign trade will equal
twenty-three millions sterling.

We not only then have rights in Manchuria,
but considerable and increasing interests arising
out of those rights.

At the beginning of the present year, when
Mr. Curzon was speaking in the House of
Commons of the necessity of maintaining these
rights and interests, the Leader of the Opposition
asked if they were threatened.   It is well for
the nation thoroughly to understand that they
are.   In 1886, when Mr. James Fulford and I
travelled round Manchuria, we did not meet
with a single Russian.   Practically, the whole

trade was in the hands of British merchants,
and the only Russian we ever heard of was an
escaped convict from Siberia. The Russians
were then very reasonably in some dread of
the Chinese, and especially of a combination
of Chinese land-power with British sea-power;
for the only line of communication the Russians
had lay along the actual frontier, and was
exposed to attack for hundreds of miles, while
the railway was at that time thousands of miles
distant. The Russians for years had had the
right to navigate the Sungari River, but had
never exercised it, chiefly through fear of the
Chinese. Their commercial interests in Manchuria were absolutely *nil*, and their thoughts
at that time were chiefly centred in endeavour-
ing to secure the strip of sea-coast, including
Vladivostok, which they had already filched
from China.

Now all is changed. They have engineers
in every part of Manchuria. They have hundreds of soldiers as escort to those engineers. They are constructing railways through
the land. And they have organised a fleet for
the navigation of the inland waters. To all
this we have no possible need to raise objection.

Such action in itself is no threat to our rights and interests.   On the contrary, by opening up the country and by enriching the inhabitants, these measures will make Manchuria all the better a market for our goods.

But Russia goes further than this.   She tells us that Manchuria is to be within the sphere of Russian influence.*   She objects to our asking China to open a second Treaty Port (Talien-wan), though she sees no objection to bullying China into handing her over two ports, both of which she proceeds to fortify, and one of which she absolutely closes to trade.   She attempts to negotiate a loan with China, but when China tries to negotiate one with us, she so threatens her, that Chinese officials come piteously to us † saying that they are so afraid of Russia they cannot do business with us.   She obtains exclusive rights of railway construction in North Manchuria, but she vigorously protests ‡ against the employment by a Chinese railway company in the South of an English engineer (Kinder) who had been with that same company

* *Vide* Blue Book, China, No. 1 (1898), p. 6.
† *Vide idem*, p. 32.
‡ *Vide idem*, p. 5.

for seventeen years, and who had performed the greatest services to all civilised nations by introducing the first railway into China. Lastly, she puts such pressure on the Chinese, that, though this same Chinese railway company were in the act of ordering the necessary railway plant and materials from an English firm, under Russian threats these orders were never given; when the Company wanted to borrow money from an English bank, she actually went the length of threatening to annex a Chinese province as "compensation"!

If we may judge then from the recent experiences of our minister at Peking, from the experience of other British representatives in different parts of Asia, and, I may add, from my own experiences, we may expect that the Russian agents on this spot will in the future, as in the past, deliberately set themselves, by open means or underhand, by hook or by crook to undermine British influence, to check the spread of British commerce, and to crush out British trade wherever that is possible. Personally and individually, Russians are the most charming people in the world. In spite of their reputation for prevarication they are frank and they are kindly and warm-hearted. But I do not think they would deny—those whom I have met have openly admitted — that politically, their object is to extend their influence over all the countries bordering on their Asiatic Empire, and wherever their influence has been extended to exclude British trade. The policy of the open door finds favour with us because we can beat the Russians in commercial competition. But the Russians prefer the door closed, with themselves inside, and us on the outside. They think that then they have a better chance.

Moreover, in pursuing this policy of absorption and exclusion, they are not afraid to resort to bluff of the most audacious kind. Their advance towards Herat, on to the Pamirs and to Port Arthur, has in each case been carried out by pure unmitigated bluff. And to one who saw them, as I did, scarcely a dozen years ago, crouching behind the Amur frontier in scarcely disguised terror lest the Chinese by land from Manchuria, and ourselves by sea from Port Hamilton, should quietly close the pincers and nip off Vladivostok, the audacity of their coolly asking the Chinese to deliver up their chief naval base, of their asking us to remove our ships from it before it was even theirs, and of their then walking into it in the face of a powerful British fleet, seems astounding beyond all expression.

With these facts before us, we cannot doubt that our rights *are* threatened, and that if some period is not put to the tide of Russian aggressiveness, all our privileges in Manchuria will be swept away. We may still enjoy those indirect advantages which the substitution of Russian for Chinese civilisation in Manchuria will bring about, just as we enjoy certain advantages from the substitution of Russian for Turkish rule in Batoum. But we will not enjoy the full advantages to which we are entitled. If the Russians continue to hold the same ideas of expansion, and to carry them out with the same audacity and determination as heretofore, in a score or so of years Manchuria will be absorbed by Russia, and British trade will be excluded.

And what if it is? some will say. After all, our trade with Manchuria never will be more than a small fraction of the total trade of the British Empire, and would it be worth while for the preservation of that to run the risk of a war with Russia?

My reply would be that it is not merely for
the sake of the £ s. d. that we would strive to
maintain our present position. We should do
so to uphold a principle—the principle that,
while we are prepared to respect the rights of
others, we are equally determined to maintain
our own. In India we know perfectly well the
absolute necessity of not giving way on a point
of principle before an Asiatic power. In the
matter of Manchuria we are engaged with
two Asiatic powers, Russia and China, each
of whom it is necessary to treat on precisely
the same lines. Give way an inch before an
Asiatic, and he believes you weak, increases in
bombast, and gives you infinite trouble afterwards, when you are compelled to make clear
to him your true relative position. Give way
upon a question of our rights in Manchuria
without obtaining some counterbalancing advantage, and we shall have a compound increase
of difficulties afterwards in maintaining similar
rights, first in North China, and afterwards
in the Yangtse Valley; for not only will the
Russians have less compunction about infringing
our rights, but they will also be in a better
position for enforcing their demands.

How, then, are we to preserve our rights? No one who has moved about in Asia can doubt that we and the Russians are in a state of rivalry. Every year we come closer together in one part of Asia or the other. It is supremely important that we should meet in peace. An honourable understanding between the two powers, defining their respective interests and the guarantees for maintaining them would be of incalculable advantage to both. But such an understanding would be absolutely worthless if the Russians had any reason to believe that it was sought for by us merely through fear of them. It can only be of value when the Russians on their part have realised the need of it. This they apparently do not realise at present, and our recent attempts to come to an understanding with them proved futile.

We can therefore either meet their bluff with bluff on our part, as Beaconsfield did in moving Indian troops to Malta, or else we can continue our policy of countermoves. We have declared ourselves against the policy of bluff as being too risky. There remains the policy of countermoves. The Russian move towards Herat has probably been more than counteracted by the strong defensive measures we have taken in the direction of Kandahar. The Russian advance to the Pamirs has certainly been fully counterbalanced by our moves to Hunza and Chitral. Perhaps we may hope that the acquisition of Wei-hai-wei will form a due reply to the Russian lease of Port Arthur. In this way only does it seem possible to prevent the Russians acquiring that political influence which we have so much reason to fear may be exercised to the detriment of our commercial interests.

There is indeed one other method which many advocate for the purpose of staying the advance of Russian influence. It is the policy of bolstering up China. But before we adopt that policy, I think we ought to consider with the utmost attention what it really means. In Turkey, in Persia, in Afghanistan, we have tried a similar policy; we have tried to infuse life into moribund semi-civilised states, and in our selfish interests to use them as buffers against the advance of civilisation. But we have had but small success. After spending millions of money and thousands of lives in support of Turkey, we had very nearly to go to

war with her on account of her cruel adminis-
tration.   For many years we supported Persia
with officers, money and arms, but when Russia
attacked the northern provinces we did not
think it worth while to support Persia sufficiently
to prevent her taking them, and we eventually
had to go to war with Persia ourselves.   And
in regard to Afghanistan we should, I am sure,
like to be a good deal more certain than we are
that all the money and patience we have spent
upon it have not been thrown away.

On the other hand, wherever either ourselves
or the Russians have assumed control over
semi-civilised states, progress and improvement
have invariably resulted, and, taken as a whole,
our respective positions have been strengthened,
not weakened.   We are not weaker for our
advance through India, and the Russians are
not weaker for their advance into the Caucasus
and Central Asia.   At the same time the people
in both are better off than they have ever been
before.

We should then take into consideration the
almost irresistible tendency of the times for the
civilised nations of Europe to control the less
civilised peoples of Asia.   Still more seriously

should we regard the strong moral conviction which is growing up that in these days of over-crowding the resources of the rich portions of the earth cannot be allowed to run to waste in the hands of semi-civilised peoples who will not develop them.

These tendencies we have to reckon with, and if we decide that it is imprudent to oppose them, then we must desist from our policy of supporting uncivilised against civilised people. We must be true to ourselves, and trust our own strength, and if combinations of European Powers are brought against us, secure a European, or still better an American ally, on our side. Executive ministers, with the great weight of a huge empire on them, no doubt have all our little weak points sparkling in their eyes; and the strength of our opponents looms large before them. They shrink from any possible risk, and are inclined to clutch on to the nearest person who can assist them, and the nearest person is the one who is also threatened. But our enemy, when viewed at close quarters, is very far from being so strong as he looks from London. He makes a brave show to impress people, but he is perfectly well aware himself that there are some very nasty chinks in his armour.   And he knows, too, that there are others around him who would be only too glad to trip him up from behind.

If Russia absorbs China bit by bit, and at the same time regards our interests, we should be only too thankful; for the substitution of Russian for Mandarin government could in that case be nothing but advantageous   If Russia comes with an ally and attempts to absorb China for herself, regardless of our interests, as she at present seems inclined to do, then we also must bring up an ally on our side, to assist us in the protection of common interests.   There are other nations besides ourselves interested in seeing that China does not become exclusively Russian, and among them it ought to be possible to find an ally. All I would urge from my experience of Asiatic countries is that the ally should be white, and not yellow; that we should not expend our resources in supporting a party who is incapable of supporting himself; that we should rather spend these resources in strengthening ourselves.

Perhaps, then, we may be permitted to hope

that in the long years to come, while we
ourselves more fully realise that supporting
decayed empires in our selfish interests is
eventually detrimental to those interests, the
Russians on their side will recognise that the
action of selfishly excluding us from countries
they have absorbed recoils upon themselves
from the opposition it naturally engenders in
us. Let us desist from bolstering up effete
states in opposition to the Russians, and not
fear to extend our control where circumstances
have made this imperative, to be timid when
we see the Russians doing likewise ; and let the
Russians give up their present policy of jealously
excluding our trade from the countries they
control.

Then, and only then, will it be possible to
effect that understanding between our great
rivals and ourselves, to attain which must ever
be the goal of our endeavours.

I have shown that Manchuria is a valuable
country ; that we have rights and interests in
it ; that those rights have been threatened by
Russia, and will probably be so threatened in
the future, and that if our rights are not rigidly

upheld in Manchuria, our task in afterwards
upholding them in North China and the
Yangtse Valley will be doubly increased. I
have assumed that in these days of hungry
competition among the nations it is even more
difficult than before to support a weak uncivilised state against the advance of European
Powers, and that when the former owns un-
developed estates, the exploitation of which is
of vital importance to mankind in general, to
attempt to impede that advance is scarcely less
immoral than futile. The problem, then, has
been how to preserve our interests without
pig-headedly impeding the legitimate advance of
Russia. The solution I offer is, that finding it
impossible at present to come to an understanding with her, we must exert our energies
to compel her to come to such an agreement—
not, however, by supporting China to resistance,
but by making Russia realise that advances on
her part which are accompanied by the exclusion of British trade and the cancelment of our
rights, only necessitate counter-advances on our
side; that we cannot possibly sit still and see
our trade driven out of country after country,
province after province, and port after port.

In this view we must give up our House of
Commons ideas on preserving the integrity of
China. We gave them up in practice, almost
as soon as the Resolution of last February was
passed, and under the pressure of circumstances
we annexed Wei-hai-wei and Mir's Bay. We
must, instead, remember that there are greater
forces than our individual wills which rule the
world, and that however fixedly we may make
up our minds to do one thing, we are often
driven by those forces to do precisely the
opposite. From the beginning of the history
of mankind there has been a force engendered
by rivalry and competition, first impelling barbarous man to clear out the beast of the field
from the best parts of the earth, then, driving
on the more advanced to subdue the barbarous,
and now urging the civilised either to oust or
control the uncivilised.

That force it is which has caused the progress
of the world, which has placed the strong above
the weak, the good above the bad, which
compelled a trading company, much against its
own will, to take the whole of India, to our
ultimate advantage and the good of the world,
and which is driving us and other European

nations upon the borders of China, as will turn
out to the eventual benefit both of the Chinese
themselves and of the rest of mankind.

To give way to that force, many think to be
immoral.   But that force acts in accordance
with the laws of the world, and is the means of
progress.   The immorality is surely rather in
opposing it, by upholding the unfit nations of
the earth against the fit, and so impeding the
onward trend of civilisation.

Probably no Government would act on the
lines above suggested.   British Governments
can only afford to look at the immediate
present, and act as pays best at the moment.
And the propping up of China seems to give
promise of averting danger for a time.   But
posterity will find that the words herein set
forth are just and true, and that our soundest
policy is to look to ourselves and to white
allies.

CHAPTER V.

PEKING TO THE GOBI DESERT.

"And o'er him many changing scenes must roll,
Ere toil his thirst for travel can assuage."

—*Byron.*

To return to the narrative of my travels,
while I was waiting in Peking news arrived
that Colonel M. S. Bell, V.C., of the Royal
Engineers, was to come there and travel thence
straight through overland to India. I knew
Colonel Bell, having served under him in the
Intelligence Department in India, so I immediately decided upon asking him to allow
me to accompany him. Here was the opportunity for which I had longed. Here was a
chance of visiting that hazy mysterious land
beyond the Himalayas, and actually seeing
Kashgar and Yarkand, with whose names I
had been acquainted from my boyhood through
the letters of my uncle, Robert Shaw. A

journey overland to India would take us through the entire length of Chinese Turkestan, the condition of which was still unknown since the Chinese had reconquered it by one of those long-sustained efforts for which they are so remarkable. We should be able to see those secluded people of Central Asia, dim figures of whom I had pictured in my mind from reading the accounts of the few travellers who had been amongst them.

Then, too, there was the fascination of seeing the very heart of the Himalayas, as we should have to cross their entire breadth on the way to India. And all combined was one grand project—this idea of striking boldly out from Peking to penetrate to India—that of itself inspired enthusiasm and roused every spark of exploring ardour in me. No excitement I have ever experienced has come up to that of planning out a great journey. The only drawback in such a life is the subsequent reaction when all is over, and the monotonous round of ordinary existence oppresses one by its torpidity and flatness in comparison. The project before me was a journey in length nearly as great as one across Central Africa and back again, and, to me at least, far more interesting than any African travel—a journey through countries varying from the level wastes of the Gobi Desert to the snow-clad masses of the Himalayas; passing, moreover, through the entire length of an empire with a history of three thousand years behind it, and still fresh in interest to the present day. And with the chance of making such a journey who could help feeling all the ardent excitement of travel rising in him, and long to be started on it?

Colonel Bell arrived in Peking towards the end of March, and to my delight said he would be only too glad to allow me to accompany him; but he thought that it would be a waste of energy for two officers to travel together along the same road, so we arranged to follow different routes.

There were, of course, initial difficulties to be overcome—the chief one being the obtaining leave of absence from my regiment. But Sir John Walsham, for whose kindness on this occasion I could never feel too grateful, overcame this by telegraphing direct to Lord Dufferin, then Viceroy of India, and that diffi-

culty—generally the greatest which military
explorers have to encounter—was at once removed.

Colonel Bell and I meanwhile spread out
our maps and discussed operations. He was
anxious to see the more populated parts of
China in order to be the better, able to judge
of its condition and resources, and so decided
upon going through the provinces inside of
the Great Wall to Kansu, and then striking
across the Gobi Desert to Hami, following
throughout the main route between Peking
and Chinese Turkestan. To my lot fell the
newer and more purely exploring work, and
it was determined that I should follow the
direct road across the Gobi Desert, and, if
possible, meet Colonel Bell at Hami on the
opposite end.* He then left Peking, after
fixing a date for our meeting at Hami. My
friends in the Legation said that, judging

* This route had never previously, nor, as far as I am
aware, has it since been, traversed by a European. It lies
midway between the high road to Chinese Turkestan and
the route which the late Mr. Ney Elias followed in 1872 on
his way from Peking to Siberia, and for the exploration of
which he obtained the Gold Medal of the Royal Geographical Society.

from the general style of his movements, they thought it extremely improbable that he would wait for me there more than three-quarters of an hour. As it turned out, we never met again till we arrived in India, and then Colonel Bell told me that he really had waited for me a whole day in Hami—this place in the middle of Central Asia, nearly two thousand miles from our starting-point—and, astonished at finding I had not arrived punctual to time, had proceeded on his way to India!

Meanwhile I had to remain in Peking to await the reply of the telegram to the Viceroy, and occupy myself in sundry preparations, and in the search for an interpreter. A favourable reply arrived, and then Sir John Walsham, with his usual kindness, interested himself in procuring for me the best passport it was possible to obtain from the Chinese, and, having been successful, April 4, 1887, was fixed as the date of my departure from Peking.

The evening preceding was one which it will be hard indeed to forget, and I think I then for the first time clearly realised what I was undertaking. Lady Walsham asked me after dinner to mark for her on a map the

H

route I proposed to follow, and to tell her
exactly what I hoped to do. Then, as I
traced out a pencil line along the map of
Asia, I first seemed to appreciate the task
I had before me. Everything was so vague.
Nowhere in Peking had we been able to obtain
information about the road across the desert.
I had never been in a desert, and here were
a thousand miles or so of desert to be crossed.
Nor had we any information of the state of the
country on the other side of it. The country
was held by the Chinese, we knew, but how
held, what sort of order was preserved, and
how a solitary European traveller would be
likely to fare among the people we knew not.
Lastly, at the back of all, looming darkly in
the extremest distance, were the Himalayas,
to cross which had previously been considered
a journey in itself.

All the terrible vagueness and uncertainty
of everything impressed itself on me as I
traced that pencil line on the map. I was
indeed about to make a plunge into the unknown, and, however easy the route might
afterwards prove to future travellers, I felt
that it was this first plunging in that was the

true difficulty in the matter. Had but one traveller gone through before me; had I even now with me a companion upon whom I could rely, or one good servant whom I could trust to stand by me, the task would have seemed easy in comparison. But all was utterly dark before me, and the journey was to be made alone with a Chinese servant whom I had found in Peking.

That last night in safety and civilisation all these difficulties and uncertainties weighed heavily upon me. But with the morning they were forgotten, and they never troubled me again. The start was to be made, and the real excitement begun, and if the difficulties and uncertainties were great, the greater would be the satisfaction in overcoming them. An unalterable conviction came over me that somehow or other I should find myself in India in a few months' time.

Sir John and Lady Walsham and all the members of the Legation collected at the gateway to bid me good-bye, and, as they did so, I tried to thank them for all the many kindnesses they had shown me, and for the goodwill and interest they had taken in my plans.

There are many things one looks back to
on a journey, but few things cheered me so
much in my more dejected moments as the
vivid recollection I used to keep of what I felt
were the sincerely meant good wishes of the
friends I had left at Peking.

Then I rode out of the gateway and beyond
the walls of the city, and was fairly launched
on my journey. Just a few pangs of depression
and a few spectres of difficulties appeared at
first, and then they vanished for good ; and,
as the hard realities of the journey began to
make themselves felt, I braced myself up and
prepared to face whatever might occur, without
thinking of what was behind.

With me at starting was one Chinese servant
who had accompanied Mr. James through
Manchuria, and who was to act as interpreter,
but who afterwards gave up when we came
to the edge of the desert ; and a second,
Liu-san, who eventually travelled with me the
whole way to India, acting in turn as interpreter, cook, table-servant, groom, and carter.
He served me well and faithfully, he was
always hard-working and willing to face the
difficulties of the road ; and when I think of

all that depended on this, my single servant and companion, I cannot feel too grateful for the fidelity he showed in accompanying me.

For the first two weeks, to the edge of the desert, the baggage was carried in carts, while I rode. The day after leaving Peking we passed through the inner branch of the Great Wall at the Nankow gate, and a couple of days later reached Kalgan, where we found some very good shops, and I even bought a watch. This place does an immense trade with the Mongols, and with the caravans which start from there northwards across the desert to Siberia. But even here we could learn nothing about the route which I wished to follow across the desert, starting from Kwei-hwa-cheng, some marches further west of Kalgan. How devoid the Chinese are of anything like an instinct for geography ! Anything beyond a man's own town or the road he works on has no interest for him, and he knows nothing of it. Caravans start regularly from Kwei-hwa-cheng across the desert to Hami ; Kwei-hwa-cheng is only week's journey from Kalgan, and I again is a great trading centre ; and yet nowhere in

the place was information to be obtained of
the route by which we had to go. How
different all this is from what one sees in the
bazaars of Central Asia, where the merchants
—some from India, some from Turkestan,
some from Afghanistan, some even from Constantinople and Moscow—meet and talk over
the countries they have travelled in and the
state of the roads, so that a traveller can
always obtain a fair general idea of any
caravan route now in use!

At Kalgan I met the ex-captain of a Chinese
gunboat which had been engaged in the action
at Foochow during the Franco-Chinese war.
His was a curious story. The Chinese have
a principle that in a battle a commander must
either be victorious or else die. This man's
vessel had been moored at some distance from
the French fleet, and had consequently escaped
the fate of the rest of the Chinese ships, and
had not been blown out of the water. The
captain, seeing the day was lost, and not being
able to do anything to retrieve the disaster
with his little gunboat, had run ashore and
escaped. The Chinese Emperor, however,
considered this a most ignominious proceeding.

If the French had not killed him, he ought to have killed himself, and, as he had not done so, he was ordered into exile for life to the Mongolian border, and told to think himself fortunate that he had not been executed. And here the poor little gentleman was—very sore against his own government, but lively and cheery withal, and certainly most useful to me. He used to accompany me for hours through the bazaars, trying to get things which I wanted, or to obtain information about the road.

On April 12 we passed through the Great Wall, and entered what Marco Polo calls the land of Gog and Magog. The gateway was not imposing, consisting as it did merely of a rough framework of wood, near which was a low hut, in which dwelt a mandarin with a small guard, and in front of which were two small cannons fastened on to a piece of timber. On either side were large gaps in the wall—here only of mud—which carts or anything else might pass through.

On the 14th, we emerged from the desolate wind-swept valleys of the Yang-ho and entered the broad, open plain of Mongolia proper.

Morning broke as we appeared upon the plateau ; a faint blue haze hung over the low hills which edged the plain and stretched away in the far distance.   An extraordinary bounding sense of freedom came over me as I looked on that vast grassy plain, extended apparently without limit all round.   There was no let or hindrance—I could go anywhere, it seemed, and all nature looked bright, as if enticing me on.   Here and there in the distance could be seen collections of small dots, which, as we came nearer, proved to be herds of camels and cattle.   Numbers of larks rose on every side and brightened the morning with their singing.   Small herds of deer were frequently met with ;   bustard too were seen, while numbers of geese and duck were passing overhead in their flight northward.   The entry to Mongolia was entrancing, and the spirits of the whole party rose as we marched cheerily over the plains.

Away in the distance we had seen some black spots from which faint columns of blue smoke were rising peacefully in the morning air.   These were the yurts, or felt tents, of the Mongols, towards which we were making.

On arrival I found them to be very much what books of travel had led me to expect—dome-shaped, made of a framework of lattice, with felt bound round on the outside, and with a hole in the roof. The inhabitants of one of them made room for me. A felt was spread out to lie on, and a couple of small tables placed by my side. All round the sides of the tent boxes and cupboards were neatly arranged, and at one end were some vases and images of Buddha. In the centre was the fireplace, situated directly beneath the hole in the roof. I was charmed with the comfort of the place. The Chinese inns, at which I had so far had to put up, were cold and draughty. Here the sun came streaming in through the hole in the top, and there were no draughts whatever. Nor was there any dust; and this being the tent of a well-to-do Mongol, it was clean and neatly arranged.

The whole family collected to see my things, and pulled my kit to pieces. The sponge was a great source of wonder; but what attracted them most of all was a concave shaving-mirror, which magnified and contorted the face in a marvellous way. The Mongols shrieked with laughter, and made the young girls look at their faces in it, telling them they need not be proud of their good looks, as that was what they were really like.

It was a pleasure to be among these jolly, round-faced, ruddy-cheeked Mongols, after living amongst the unhealthy-looking Chinese of the country through which we had lately been travelling, who showed little friendliness or good-humour, and who always seemed to cause a bad taste in the mouth. These first Mongols happened to be an unusually attractive lot. They were, of course, better off than those whom I afterwards met with far away in the desert, and this perhaps accounted for their ever-cheery manner, which left such an agreeable impression on me.

Another attraction of this first day in Mongolia was the milk and cream—thick and rich as one would get anywhere ; and here, again, was a pleasing contrast to China, where, as I have said, the cows are never milked, and none is therefore procurable.

Altogether this was one of those bright days which throw all the hardships of travel far away into the shade, and make the traveller feel that the net result of all is true enjoyment. The shadows have only served to show up the light, and bring out more clearly the attractions of a free, roaming life.

On the following day we entered hilly country again, and at the end of the march came upon country cultivated by Chinamen, who here, as elsewhere along the borders of Mongolia, are encroaching on the Mongols, and gradually driving them out of the best country back into the desert. The slack, easy-going Mongol cannot stand before the pushing, industrious Chinaman; so back and back he goes. It is the old story which is seen all through nature—the weak and lazy succumbing to the strong and vigorous. The observer's sympathies are all with the Mongol, though, and he feels regret at seeing the cold, hard-natured Chinaman taking the place of the easy-going, open-hearted Mongol.

On arrival at Kwei-hwa-cheng on April 17, I called on Mr. and Mrs. G. W. Clarke of the China Inland Mission, to whom I had a letter of introduction. I met with that warm reception which is characteristic of missionaries; a room was prepared for me, and the most real hospitality shown me. Mr. Clarke had been established here for two years now, and was, I believe, the first permanent missionary to reside in the place. I had not before met a member of the China Inland Mission in his home, and consequently was especially interested in hearing Mr. Clarke's account of his work. The zeal and energy which this mission shows is marvellous. Its members dress as Chinamen, live right away in the interior, in the very heart of China, and make it their endeavour to get really in touch with the people. They receive no regular pay, but as money comes in to the mission, enough is sent them to cover the bare expenses of living. Often, through the lack of funds, they are on the point of starving, and Mrs. Clarke told me how, upon one occasion, she had been for two or three weeks with literally no money and no food, so that she had to beg her way and sell her clothes to raise money as best she could till money arrived from head-quarters.

Preparations for crossing the Gobi Desert to Hami, the first town in Chinese Turkestan, had now to be made. Kwei-hwa-cheng was the last town in this direction, and the starting-point

of caravans for Turkestan.   Carts, or rather
the mules or ponies which drew them, could
go no farther, so I had to discharge those I had
brought from Peking, and look out for camels.
Sallying forth to the town on the day after my
arrival, I went with Mr. Clarke to visit the
establishment of one of the great firms which
trade with Turkestan.   Here in the yards we
saw rows of neatly-bound loads of merchandise,
brick tea, cotton goods, silk, china, and iron-
mongery, all being made up ready for a caravan
which was about to start for Turkestan.   Full
information about the route was now at last
forthcoming, and I looked with the profoundest
interest on men who had actually been to these
mist-like towns of Central Asia.   It appeared
that there was a recognised route across the
desert, and that during the winter months
caravans start about once a month.

We did not at first succeed in finding a man
who was willing to hire out camels to go on
such a long journey with so small a party as
ours would be.   Men had no objection to
travelling in large caravans, but they did not
like the idea of starting across the desert with
a party of only four.   But I could not wait for

the caravan which was about to start. By
doing so I might be detained in one way and
another for some weeks, and as I had the whole
length of Chinese Turkestan to traverse, and
to cross the Himalayas before winter closed in,
I could not afford such a delay. It was fortunate for me that at this juncture I had the
aid and experience of Mr. Clarke at my disposal. He was indefatigable in his search for
a man, and eventually found a Chinese native
of Guchen who undertook to hire me out five
camels, to carry 300 lbs. each, for 180 taels
(about £45), and to provide a guide to
accompany my party across the desert to
Hami. A solemn agreement was then drawn
up, and it was stipulated that, for the above
sum, we were to be landed at Hami in sixty
days.

To consult a Chinese almanac for an
auspicious day on which to start was the
next thing. The guide was very particular
about this, as he said it would never do to start
in a casual way on a journey like this. We
must be most careful about the date of starting.
The 23rd, 24th, and 25th of April were all in
turn rejected, for one reason after another, and

the 26th was finally settled upon as being suitable in all respects.

In the meanwhile there was plenty of work to be done, laying in provisions and providing ourselves with every possible necessary. Nothing would be procurable on the way except perhaps a sheep here and there, so we had to buy up supplies of all kinds sufficient to last the party for two months. Some people think that on a journey it is absolutely necessary to make themselves as uncomfortable as possible. But I had learnt by experience to think otherwise, and determined to treat myself as well as circumstances would permit, so that, when it should become really necessary to rough it (as it afterwards did during the passage of the Himalayas), I should be fit and able to endure the hardships. So, besides a couple of sacks of flour, a sack of rice, and thirty tins of beef, which were to be our main stand-by, I had also brought from Peking such luxuries as a few tins of preserved milk, butter, and soup; and here in Kwei-hwa-cheng I procured some dried apricots and raisins, a sack of Mongolian mushrooms, which gave a most excellent relish to the soup, another sack of potatoes, a bag of dried beans, which Mr. Clarke gave me, and lastly some Chinese oatmeal. All these luxuries added very little to the total amount of baggage, and even if they had made an extra camel-load, it would not have hindered the journey in any way, while they added very considerably to my efficiency.

A tent was made up in the town on what is known in India as the Kabul pattern ; but, as it afterwards turned out, this was, for travelling in the desert, about the very worst description of tent possible. The violent winds, so constant there, catch the walls and make it almost impossible to keep the tent standing. What I would recommend for future travellers is a tent like my guide's sloping down to the ground at the ends as well as on each side, and with no straight wall to catch the wind.

Rather unusual articles of equipment were two water-casks which we filled with water daily on the march, so that if, as sometimes happened, we lost our way and missed the well, or found it choked with sand, we should always have something to fall back on.

This completed our preparations, and we were ready for the real start into the unknown.

CHAPTER VI.

ACROSS THE GOBI DESERT.

"But here—above, around, below,
  On mountain or on glen,
Nor tree, nor shrub, nor plant, nor flower,
  The weary eye may ken."
                                  —*Scott.*

THE auspicious day, April 26, having at length arrived, I had reluctantly to say good-bye to my kind and hospitable friends—the last of my countrymen I should see for many a month to come—and take my plunge into the Gobi and the far unknown beyond. We might have been starting on a voyage; all supplies for several weeks were taken, and everything made snug and ready as if going to sea. Ours was a compact little party—the camel-man, who acted as guide, a Mongol assistant, my Chinese "boy," eight camels, and myself. Chang-san, the interpreter, had gone back to Peking, feeling himself unable to face the

I

journey before us, and so I was left to get on
as best I could, in half-English, half-Chinese,
with the "boy," Liu-san. The guide was a
doubled-up little man, whose eyes were not
generally visible, though they sometimes
beamed out from behind his wrinkles and
pierced one like a gimlet. He possessed a
memory worthy of a student of Stokes, and the
way in which he remembered the position of
the wells at each march in the desert, was
simply marvellous. He would be fast asleep
on the back of a camel, leaning right over with
his head either resting on the camel's hump,
or dangling about beside it, when he would
suddenly wake up, look first at the stars, by
which he could tell the time to a quarter of an
hour, and then at as much of the country as he
could see in the dark. Having thus satisfied
himself as to our position, he would, after a
time, turn the camel a little off the track, dis-
mount, and there, sure enough, we would find
a well. The extraordinary manner in which
he kept the way surpasses anything I know of.
As a rule no track at all could be seen, especially in the sandy districts; but he used to lead
us somehow or other, generally by the tracks

of former caravans, which were so faint that I could not distinguish them even when pointed out to me, for a camel does not leave much impression upon gravel, like a beaten-down path in a garden! Another of his desert-acquired habits was that of going to sleep walking. His natural mode of progression was by bending right forward, and this seemed to keep him in motion without any trouble to himself, and he might be seen mooning along fast asleep. These were his accomplishments. His one failing was opium-smoking; directly camp was pitched he would have out his pipe, and he used to smoke off and on till we started again. I was obliged occasionally to differ with this gentleman; but, on the whole, we got on well together, and my feelings towards him at parting were more of sorrow than of anger, for he had a hard life going backwards and forwards up and down across the desert almost continuously for twenty years; and his in-veterate habit of opium-smoking had used up all the savings he ought to have accumulated after his hard experiences.

The Mongol assistant, whose name was Ma-te-la, was a careless, good-natured fellow,

always whistling or singing, and bursting into
roars of laughter at the slightest thing, especially at any little mishap! He used to think it
the best possible joke if a camel deposited one
of my boxes on to the ground and knocked the
lid off. He never ceased wondering at all my
things, and was as pleased as a child with a
new toy when I gave him an empty corned-
beef tin when he left me. That treasure of an
old tin is probably as much prized by his family
now as some jade-bowls which I brought back
from Yarkand are by mine.

Poor Ma-te-la had to do a prodigious amount
of work. He had to walk the whole—or very
nearly the whole—of each march, leading the
first camel; then, after unloading the animals,
and helping to pitch the tents, he would have
to scour the country round for the argals or
droppings of camels, which were generally all
we could get for fuel. By about two in the
morning he could probably get some sleep;
but he had to lie down amongst the camels in
order to watch them, and directly day dawned
he would get up and take them off to graze.
This meant wandering for miles and miles over
the plain, as the camels are obliged to pick up

a mouthful of scrub here and there, where they can, and consequently range over a considerable extent of ground. He would come into camp for a short time for his dinner, and then go off again, and gradually drive the camels up to be ready for the start ; then he would have to help to load them, and start off on the march. This seemed to me fearfully hard work for him, but he never appeared any the worse for it, and was always bright and cheery. I gave him a mount one day on one of my camels, but he would never get up again, as he said the guide would give him no wages if he did.

There were eight camels. I rode one myself, four others carried my baggage and stores, and my servant rode on the top of one of the baggage camels ; of the remaining three, one carried the water, one was laden with brick tea, which is used in place of money for buying things from the Mongols, and the third was loaded with the men's kit. The total weight of my baggage, with the two months' stores, servant's cooking things, camp equipage, etc., was 1416 lbs.

We left Kwei hwa-cheng by the north gate

of the town, and, after passing for some five
miles over a well-cultivated plain, began to
ascend the great buttress range on to the
Mongolian plateau. Crossing these mountains
the following day, we afterwards entered an
undulating hilly country, inhabited principally
by Chinese. Villages were numerous, cart-
tracks led in every direction, and the valleys
were well cultivated. There were also large
meadows of good grass, where immense flocks
of sheep were feeding; but I was astonished to
see that, although we were now in Mongolia,
the largest and best flocks were tended by and
belonged to Chinese, who have completely
ousted the Mongols in the very calling which,
above all, ought to be their speciality. It is
really a fact that the Chinese come all the way
from the province of Shantung to these Mongolian pasture-lands to fatten sheep for the
Peking market. Here is yet another instance
of the manner in which the pushing and industrious Chinaman is forcing his way, and
gradually driving back the less persevering
inhabitants of the country on which he en-
croaches; and it seems probable that the
Chinese from the south, and the Russians from

the north, will, in course of time, gradually force the poor Mongols into the depth of the desert.

I was warned to look out for robbers in this vicinity. Some uncanny-looking gentlemen came prowling about my camp one day, and the guide told me to keep my eye on them and have my revolver ready. But I was in some anxiety about my Chinese boy, Liusan. He knew I must have a large sum of money with me, for I was obliged to take in lumps of solid silver sufficient money to pay all my expenses as far as India, though he did not know exactly where it was, as I hid it away in all sorts of places ; one lump of silver in a sack of flour, another in an empty beef-tin, and so on. I was afraid, therefore, that if a loaded revolver were given him, he might make it very unpleasant for me one day in the wilds. So, to inspire awe of our party in outsiders, I gave him an unloaded revolver ; but afterwards, thinking that doing things by halves was of little good, I loaded the weapon for him and told him that I had the most complete trust in him. He and I must be true to each other ; I would look after him, and he must

look after me. If I came to grief he was sure
to suffer for it sooner or later. Whereas, if I
got through, a handsome reward would fall to
his lot. This method of dealing with him
answered admirably ; he used to swagger about
with the revolver, showed it to everybody he
met, and told the most abominable lies about
the execution it could do. Nobody can lie
with such good effect as a Chinaman, and as
he told the gaping Mongols and Turkis, that
though he could bowl over only about twenty
men at a time with his weapon, I had about
me much more deadly instruments, they used
to look upon me with the greatest awe, and
I never had the semblance of a disturbance on
the whole of my journey.

Liu-san's propensity for fibbing was not
always so fortunate, and he used to annoy me
considerably at times by telling people that I
was a man of great importance, with the object,
of course, of enhancing his own. I used to see
him button-hole a grave old Turki, and tell
him in a subdued whisper with mysterious
glances at me, that I was " Yăng-ta-jên," the
great man Young (husband), an influential
envoy from Peking, and that the utmost re-

spect must be shown to me. Then he would
pretend to be very obsequious, and bow and
kow-tow in the most servile manner. It was
hard to know whether to be angry with him
or to laugh; he was always so very comical.
There would be a twinkle in his eye the whole
time, and now and then, while all this panto-
mime was going on, he used to say to me in
English (*his* English), "I think master belong
big gentleman; no belong small man." He
thought I was a big gentleman quite off his
head, though, to go wandering about in such
out-of-the-way places, instead of staying comfortably at home; and he used to say, "I
think master got big heart; Chinese mandarin
no do this."

We were now gradually approaching the
heart of the Gobi, and the aspect of the
country became more and more barren; the
streams disappeared, and water could only be
obtained from the rough wells or water-holes
dug by former caravans. No grass could be
seen, and in its place the country was covered
with dry and stunted plants, burnt brown by
the sun by day and nipped by the frost by
night. Not a sound would be heard, and

scarcely a living thing seen, as we plodded along slowly, yet steadily, over those seemingly interminable plains. Sometimes I would strike off from the road, and ascend some rising ground to take a look round. To the right and left would be ranges of bare hills, very much resembling those seen in the Gulf of Suez, with rugged summits and long even slopes of gravel running down to the plain, which extended apparently without limit in front of me. And there beneath was my small caravan, mere specks on that vast expanse of desolation, and moving so slowly that it seemed impossible that it could ever accomplish the great distance which had to be passed before Hami could be reached.

Our usual plan was to start at about three in the afternoon, and travel on till midnight or sometimes later. This was done partly to avoid the heat of the day, which is very trying to the loaded camels, but chiefly to let the camels feed by daylight, as they cannot be let loose to feed at night for fear of their wandering too far and being lost. Any one can imagine the fearful monotony of those long dreary marches seated on the back of a slow and silently moving camel. While it was light I would read and even write; but soon the sun would set before us, the stars would appear one by one, and through the long dark hours we would go silently on, often finding our way by the aid of the stars alone, and marking each as it sank below the horizon, indicating how far the night was advanced. At length the guide would give the signal to halt, and the camels, with an unmistakable sigh of relief, would sink to the ground; their loads would quickly be taken off; before long camp would be pitched, and we would turn in to enjoy a well-earned sleep, with the satisfaction of having accomplished one more march on that long desert journey.

Camp was astir again, however, early in the morning, and by eight I used to get up, and after breakfast stroll about to see what was to be seen, then write up my diary, plot out the map, have dinner at one or two, and then prepare for the next march. And so the days wore on with monotonous regularity for ten whole weeks.

But though these marches were very monotonous, yet the nights were often extremely

beautiful, for the stars shone out with a magnificence I have never seen equalled even in
the heights of the Himalayas. Venus was
a resplendent object, and guided us over many
a mile of that desert. The Milky Way, too,
was so bright that it looked like a phos-
phorescent cloud, or as a light cloud with the
moon behind it. This clearness of the atmosphere was probably due to its remarkable
dryness. Everything became parched up, and
so charged with electricity, that in opening out
a sheepskin coat or a blanket a loud cracking
noise would be given out, accompanied by a
sheet of fire. A very peculiar and unlooked-
for result of this remarkable dryness of the
atmosphere was the destruction of a highly-
cherished coat which Sir John Walsham had
given me just before I left Peking, saying that
it would last me for ever ; and so it would
have done anywhere else but in the Gobi
Desert. It was made of a very closely woven
canvas material, and to all appearance was in-
destructible, but it is a fact that before a month
was over, that coat was in shreds. From the
extreme dryness it got brittle, and wherever
creases were formed, it broke in long rents.

A NIGHT MARCH IN THE GOBI DESERT.

Page 124.

The outside bend of the elbow of the sleeve was as sound as on the day it was bought, but the *inside* of the bend was cut to pieces, and split wherever it had been creased by the elbow.

The temperature used to vary very considerably. Frosts continued to the end of May, but the days were often very hot, and were frequently hottest at nine or ten in the morning, for later on a strong wind would usually spring up, blowing sometimes with extreme violence, up till sunset, when it generally subsided again. If this wind was from the north, the weather was fine but cold. If it was from the south, it would be warmer, but clouds would collect and rain would sometimes fall ; generally, however, the rain would pass off into steam before reaching the ground. Ahead of us we would see rain falling heavily, but before it reached the ground it would gradually disappear—vanish away—and when we reached the spot over which the rain had apparently been falling, there would not be a sign of moisture on the ground.

The daily winds, of which I have just spoken, were often extremely disagreeable.

It was with the greatest difficulty that we could keep our tents from being blown down, and everything used to become impregnated with the sand, which found its way everywhere, and occasionally we had to give up our march because the camels could not make any head against the violence of the wind.

Every evening about five we would see herds and flocks slowly wending their way over the plain and converging on the water near the camp, but only the sheep seemed to be attended by any one, and there was scarcely ever a tent in sight.

The ponies went about in a semi-wild state, in troops of about twenty mares, under the guardianship of one or more stallions, who drove them about from place to place seeking something to graze on.   They were entirely free, and every evening at sunset they marched slowly back to the Mongol yurt.

But the desert had also its charms, and on the mornings when there was a lull in the terrific storms, no artist could wish for a finer display of colouring than the scene then presented.   Overhead would be a spotless, clear blue sky, and beneath it the plain lost its dull monotonous aspect, fading away in various shades of blue, each getting deeper and deeper, till the hills were reached ; and these again, in their rugged outline, presented many a pleasing variety of colour, all softened down with a hazy bluish tinge ; while the deceitful mirage made up for the absence of water in the scene, and the hills were reflected again in what appeared to be lovely lakes of clear, still water.

The Bortson well was reached on May 22. Here were a few Mongol yurts on the banks of some small trickles of water, running down from the Hurku Hills to the north ; and it was at this point that I crossed the track of the Russian traveller, Prjevalsky. In his first, and also in his third journey, he had crossed the Galpin Gobi from the south, and passed through this place on his way northward to Urga. Describing the Galpin Gobi at this point, the great Russian traveller says : " This desert is so terrible that, in comparison with it, the deserts of Northern Tibet may be called fruitful. There, at all events, you may find water and good pasturage in the valleys : here there is neither, not even a single oasis—everywhere the silence of the Valley of Death. The Hurku Hills are the northern definition of the wildest and most sterile part of the Gobi."

After this we crossed some low hills running down from the Hurku range, and arrived on the banks of a little stream, about a foot wide and a few inches deep, with small patches of green grass on its margin, where we halted for three days to buy a couple of new camels. There were several Mongol yurts about, and we had visits from some of the men. They were tall, strong, muscular fellows, but very childish, amused at everything, and very rough in their manners.

Looking on these uncouth, indolent men, it was difficult to imagine that they were the descendants of the wild Tartar hordes, who under Chengiz Khan had conquered China, had penetrated to India, had subdued all Turkestan and Persia, and swept through Russia even to Central Europe. I had now seen Mongols in the far eastern end of Mongolia, where Chengiz Khan first commenced to establish his control over them. I had seen them in those districts round the Great Wall where he led them on his first incursion into China proper, and I now

saw them in those remoter desert tracts through
which they again and again passed in their
marches westward.   Had these Mongols degenerated from what they once had been?
Were they the mere embers of a fiery race?
and was that fire latent or extinct?   These
were questions which often puzzled me as I
looked on the dirty ragged individual who
came begging to me and went away satisfied
when my servants gave them brown paper for
tobacco, and old lime-juice bottles as valuable
presents.

On reading over the accounts of the Mongols
in the zenith of their power, I see no reason to
think that those who followed Chengiz Khan
were so very different from those I saw to-day.
Dull, heavy, and indolent as these latter are,
they have at any rate the attribute of hardiness.
They are still capable, by living on the fermented
milk of mares, called kumiss, of carrying out
prodigious marches.   And they are probably
to-day just as capable of committing the barbarous cruelties for which they were famous as
they were in the days of Chengiz. The great
mass of the Mongols are probably very much
the same to-day as they were at the time of the

K

Crusades, when they were establishing a power in Asia, the last remnant of which only disappeared with the Moghal Emperor at Delhi in 1857.

What fused this inert mass into so vivid a life, was the genius of one great man. Unscrupulous, treacherous, and pitilessly cruel, Chengiz Khan undoubtedly was, but he had to a supreme degree, that vital energy which in one direction irresistibly attracted men to him, and in another direction crushed down everything before it. Driven by this fiery force, the Mongols were hurled forth over Asia as from a volcano. The eruption subsided, and to-day only the bare crater is visible. Whether the volcano is altogether extinct, time only can show. It may after centuries of quiescence break out again. But certainly now there is no indication of such an eventuality, and anything less dangerous than these listless nomads, it would be hard to conceive.

Two new camels having been purchased, we set out again on the 28th, in spite of the violent wind that was blowing; but we did not get far, and had to halt again the whole of the next day on account of the wind. Although it was now the end of May, the cold at night was still considerable, and I have noted that in bed I wore two flannel shirts and a cardigan jacket, lying under two thick blankets. It was the wind that made it cold, blowing from the W.N.W. and N.W.

On June 3, just as we were preparing to start, we saw a great dark cloud away in the distance over the plain. It was a dust storm coming towards us. Where we were it was quite still, and the sky was bright overhead, and perfectly clear, but away to the west we saw the dark clouds — as black as night. Gradually they overspread the whole sky, and as the storm came nearer we heard a rumbling sound, and then it burst upon us with terrific force, so that we were obliged to lie at full length on the ground behind our baggage. There was fortunately no sand about—we were on a gravel plain—but the small pebbles were being driven before the wind with great velocity, and hurt us considerably. The storm lasted for half an hour, and it was then as calm and bright as before, and much cooler.

A few days later we crossed a ridge connecting the Hurku Hills with the southern range, and descended a wide valley or plain between those two ranges on the western side of the connecting ridge. Between us and the southern range was a most remarkable range of sandhills, called by my guide Hun-kua-ling. It was about forty miles in length, and composed of bare sand, without a vestige of vegetation of any sort on it, and I computed it in places to be as much as nine hundred feet in height, rising abruptly out of a gravel plain. With the dark outline of the southern hills as a background, this white fantastically shaped sand-range presented a very striking appearance. It must have been formed by the action of the wind, for to the westward is an immense sandy tract, and it is evident that the wind has driven the sand from this up into the hollow between the Hurku Hills and the range to the south, thus forming these remarkable sandhills.

After passing the end of the sand-range, we entered a country different from any we had yet been through. In the stage of its evolution previous to the present it was probably a plain of sand. But the elements of the air seem to have fought with and rent the very surface of the land, torn it up and tossed it about, here

SANDHILLS IN THE GOBI DESERT.

Page 132.

furrowing out depressions, there piling up fantastic sandhills, while, to add to the weirdness of the spectacle, the country was covered with tamarisk bushes, the roots of which had been laid bare by the wind blowing the sand away, till they stood everywhere with their gnarled and contorted roots exposed to view. The sandhills were sometimes very quaint and curious in shape, but they usually ran in long ridges, cutting into one another from every direction.

I suggested to the guide that we should halt for a day when we came to a good grazing-ground, to let the camels pick up, and then make a renewed effort to reach Hami; but he said that if they were to halt for one day, they would not go on at all the next—the only thing was to keep them at it. Rather like the cab-horse in 'Pickwick,' which had to be kept in harness for fear of it falling down!

The Altai Mountains, rising to a height of about nine thousand feet above the sea, and covered with slight snow on the summit, now lay about twenty-five miles to the north. They were entirely bare, and the southern slopes were steep, but not precipitous. In the centre of the range is said to be a plateau of grass land to which the wild camels resort. The guide told me the wild camels keep away from the caravan tracks and stay up in the mountains. The Mongols follow them there and catch their young, which they use for riding only, as the camels will not carry a pack. Their legs are thin, and the hair smooth. At three years old they are said to be of the size of a horse; at five years, the size of a small tame camel.

The guide also said that there were wild horses and what he called mules from this district westward. I saw some of the so-called wild mules through my telescope. They are the kyang or wild asses of Ladak and Tibet, and are in size about thirteen or fourteen hands, and in colour a light bay, being brightest under the belly. The head and tail were like a mule's, the neck thick and arched. They trotted fast, with a free, easy motion. The guide says the horses go about in troops of two or three hundred.

One evening Ma-te-la, the Mongol assistant, was suddenly seen to shoot ahead at a great pace, and, on asking, I found he was going home. On he went, far away over the plain,

till he became a mere dot in the distance. I
could not help envying him, for in the same
direction, and with nothing apparently between
me and it but distance, was *my* home, and I felt
myself struggling to pierce through space, and
see myself returning, like Ma-te-la, home. But
the dull reality was that I was trudging along
beside a string of heavy, silent, slow-going
camels, and on I had to go, for hour after hour
through the night with monotonous regularity.

Suddenly, after travelling for nine hours, the
gravel plain ended, and we passed over a stretch
of grass and halted by a small stream. Close
by were pitched four tents (yurts), and this was
Ma-te-la's home.

The same evening I noted a very remarkable
sunset. Sunsets in the desert are always bright
and glowing and rich in colour. But even in
the Indian hills during the rains I have never
seen such a peculiar tinge as the clouds showed
that night. It was not red, it was not purple,
but a mixture between the two—very deep,
and at the same time shining very brightly. I
have seen at Simla and in Switzerland more
glorious sunsets, with richer diffusion and
variety of colours, but never one of such a

strange lurid colouring as this. An hour and a half later, when it was nearly dark, a very light, phosphorescent-looking cloud hung over the place where the sun had gone down.

So we plodded on night after night over the desert, and halting for the day sometimes by the side of a minute little streamlet, where we would find a few Mongols encamped, more often by a roughly-dug waterhole, in the midst of a desert with not a sign of human habitation in sight. At last, one evening, towards the end of June, when, after two months of desert travel my patience was well-nigh exhausted, a ray of light appeared. I had climbed one of the highest hills to have a look round. There were plenty of white soft clouds about, but suddenly my eye rested on what I felt sure must be something more than a mere cloud and must be a great snowy range. I had out my telescope in a moment, and there, in truth, far away in the distance, only just distinguishable from the clouds, were real snow mountains. These could be none other than the Tian-shan; my delight was unbounded, and long did I feast my eyes on those " Heavenly Mountains," as the Chinese name them, for

they belonged to Turkestan and marked the
end of my long desert journey, and the con-
clusion of one great stage on the way to
India.

Our next march, however, was the most
trying of all, for we had to cross the branch of
the Gobi which is called the desert of Zungaria,
one of the most absolutely sterile parts of the
whole Gobi.   We started at eleven in the
morning, passing at first through the low hills,
perfectly barren for the most part, though some
hollows had a few tufts of bushes, and one
hollow was filled with white roses.   After
seven and a half miles we left the hills, and
entered a gravel plain covered with coarse
bushes, but no grass.   There was no path, and
we simply headed straight for the end of the
Tian-shan range.   Through the whole afternoon we pressed wearily along.   Sunset, and
still we did not halt, for there was no water
for many miles ahead.   At last, near midnight,
we halted for a time over the plain to cook
some food and rest the camels.   To pitch
camp was useless, for there was neither water,
fuel, nor grass; not a bush, nor a plant, nor a
blade of grass—absolutely nothing but gravel

as bare as a well-kept garden drive. I lay
down on the ground and slept till Liu-san
brought me some soup and tinned beef. We
started again at four, watched the sun rise
again, marched through the whole morning
right up to three in the afternoon, passing over
the most desolate country I have ever seen.
Nothing we had passed hitherto could compare
with it—a succession of gravel ranges without
a sign of life, animal or vegetable, and not a
drop of water. We were gradually descending
to a very low level, the sun was getting higher
and higher, and the wind hotter and hotter,
until I shrank from it as from the blast of a
furnace, and would often put my hand up to
shield my face. Only the hot winds of the
Punjab could be likened to it.

Fortunately we still had some water in the
casks, brought from our last camping-ground,
and we had some bread, so we were not on
our last legs ; but the march was trying enough
for the men, and much more so for the camels,
for they had nothing to eat or drink, and the
heat both days was extreme. The guide called
the distance two hundred and thirty li, and I
reckon it at about seventy miles. We were

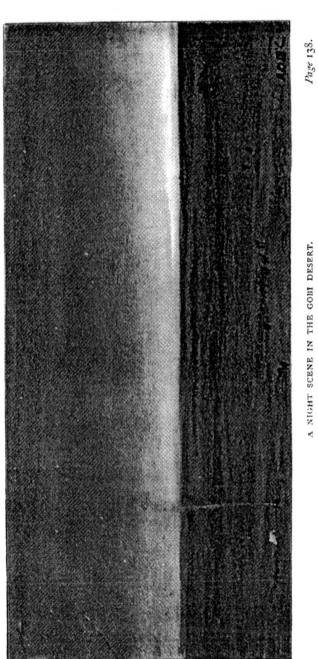

A NIGHT SCENE IN THE GOBI DESERT.

Page 138.

twenty-seven hours and three-quarters from camp, including the halt of four and a half hours. We had descended nearly four thousand feet, and the heat down here was very much greater than we had yet experienced. We encamped near a well on the dry bed of a river, on the skirts of what looked like a regular park—the country being covered with trees, and the ground with long coarse grass. It was most striking, as on the other bank of the river there was not a vestige of vegetation.

After this long and trying march we (or I at any rate) obtained scarcely a wink of sleep, for the heat was stifling, there was not a breath of air, and I was lying on the ground in a Kabul tent pestered by a plague of sandflies, which found their way into my eyes, nose, and everywhere. That was the most despairing period of my whole journey, and many times that night I bewailed my folly, and swore by all the gods I would never wander about the wild places of the earth again. These periods of depression must occur to every traveller. He cannot help now and then asking himself "What's the good of it all? Why should I leave all the comforts of civilised life and deliberately place myself amid depressing surroundings, and of my own free will go through such hardships?" But 'tis always darkest before the dawn, and I could just see the first glimmering of awakening day—the snowy summits of the "Heavenly Mountains" were rising above me. The desert journey was nearly at an end, and before long we should be among a new people and passing through towns and villages again.

Impatient to reach the promised land as soon as our well-nigh worn-out camels would carry us thither, we made an early start the next day. For nearly two miles we passed through a country well covered with trees, and patches of coarse grass and bushes, growing on a soil partly clay and partly sand. This unusual vegetation ended as suddenly as it had begun, and we passed over the gravel desert again, where there was no vestige of either grass or scrub. The hot wind blowing off this seemed absolutely to scorch one up; but yesterday's order of things was now reversed —we were ascending while the sun was descending, and it gradually became cooler,

as afternoon passed into evening, and as we
slowly climbed the long even slopes of the
Tian-shan.

About ten at night we suddenly found ourselves passing over turf, with bushes and trees
on either side ; a shrill clear voice hailed us
from out of the darkness. The guide answered,
and a Turki woman then appeared, who led us
through the bushes over some cultivated ground
to a house—the first I had seen for nearly a
thousand miles, and the first sign that I had
entered Turkestan—the mysterious land which
I had longed for many a day to see.

Flowing by the house was a little stream of
clear, fresh water. It was scarcely a yard
broad, but it was not a mere trickle like the
others we had passed in the Gobi, it was
flowing rapidly, with a delightful gurgling noise,
and was deep enough for me to scoop up
water between my two hands. I gulped down
mouthful after mouthful of the delicious liquid,
and enjoyed such a drink as I had not had for
many a long day, and as I lay down on the
grass on its bank while the water-casks were
being filled, I thought the trials of the desert
journey were nearly over and that some few

comforts and fresh interests were near at hand.

As we now ascended the range the slopes were covered with rich green turf, most delightful to look upon after the bare hills of the Gobi ; while here and there through an opening in the hills we could catch a glimpse of the snowy peaks above. There were, however, no trees nor even bushes, either on the hills or in the valleys. By the roadside we passed several horns of the *Ovis argali*, and two other kinds of wild sheep or goat, *Ovis argali* being the most common. One of these measured 56 inches and another 62 inches in length. The latter, the guide said, was as big a one as was to be got.

All the *Ovis argali* horns I saw on the Tian-shan were different from those which I saw on the Altai Mountains. The latter were thicker at the base (nineteen inches round as against sixteen), and they were more rounded, and not so much twisted. The Mongol says the sheep are the same.

We crossed the Tian-shan at a height of eight thousand feet. Except the last half-mile the ascent was not steep, but led gradually up

FARM IN THE TIAN-SHAN MOUNTAINS.

Page 141.

a narrow valley. The last mile or two was over soft green turf, and near the summit there was a perfect mass of flowers, chiefly forget-me-nots ; and the sight of all this rich profusion of flowers and grass, in place of the dreary gravel slopes of the Gobi Desert, was a treat to be remembered.

Yet there were still no trees to be seen, and a curious characteristic of these hills was their entire want of water. For twelve miles from Morgai to the summit of the pass we had not seen a drop. From this absence of water the valleys were not deep—not more than five or six hundred feet below the summit of the hills on either side—nor were the hillsides remarkably steep, as in the Himalayas. They were grassy slopes with rocks cropping out at their summits, and here and there on their sides. But five miles on the southern side a small stream appeared, and the valley bottom was partitioned off into fields, round which irrigation ducts had been led. Trees now at last began to appear, and we pitched camp on a little grassy plot near a stream of cold clear water, and under a small grove. Such a treat I had not enjoyed for many a long day. I

seemed to be in a perfect paradise, and the
desert journey appeared a terrible nightmare
behind me. The signs of life all round so striking after the death-like silence of the desert,
lightened me as a breath of fresh air. The
twittering of the birds and the hum of insects
in comparison with the quiet of the Gobi,
appeared like London's central roar, and I felt
myself once again to be amid animate nature.
Vegetation too was everywhere more abundant
now, and on the northern slopes of some of the
hills I even saw patches of pine forests.

On July 22 we passed a small square-walled
town called Ching-cheng, surrounded by fields
of wheat and some good grass land ; but when
these ended the desert began again directly.

A long way off over the desert we could see
a couple of poplar trees rising out of the plain,
which I fondly hoped might be Hami, our
destination. We reached these at twelve at
night, and found a few soldiers stationed there,
who said that Hami was still far distant. Now,
as my constant inquiry for the last month had
been, " How far are we from Hami ? " and as
the guide for the last few days had each time
said we were only sixty miles distant, I was

exasperated to find that, instead of having ten or twenty miles more to accomplish, there was still a good fifty. So on striking camp at two the following afternoon, I told my men that my tent would not be pitched again till Hami was reached, and they had better prepare themselves therefore for a good march.

We travelled on all through the afternoon—a particularly hot one; then the sun set before us, and still we went on and on through the night till it rose again behind us. We halted for a couple of hours by the roadside to ease the camels, and then set out again. At eight o'clock the desert ended, and we began to pass through cultivated land. At last we saw Hami in the distance, and after traversing a tract of country covered with more ruined than inhabited houses, we reached an inn at 11 A.M.

With unspeakable relief I dismounted from my camel for the last time. The desert journey was now over, and I had completed the 1255 miles from Kwei-hwa-cheng in just seventy days; in the last week of which I had travelled 224 miles, including the crossing of the Tian-shan Mountains. One great stage

L

in my journey through to India was accomplished.   The dreariness and dangers of the desert were left behind, and new experiences, new races of men, new modes of travelling and changing types of country now lay before me.

CHAPTER VII.

THROUGH TURKESTAN TO YARKAND.

MY first inquiries on arrival were as to whether Colonel Bell had arrived. I had reached Hami some weeks later than the date on which, in the Legation at Peking, we had fixed to meet here, but still he had had a long round to travel, and might have been late too. I was disappointed to find that he had passed through about three weeks before, and must now be well on his way to India.

My next inquiries were as to the means of reaching Kashgar, the principal town at the western extremity of Turkestan, and the time it would take to reach there. The result of the inquiries was unsatisfactory. Difficulties, of course, arose. It was the hot season, and carters would not hire out their carts. In any case it would take seventy days to reach there, and this would bring us to the end of September, with the whole of the Himalayas to cross before winter.

However, I left all such matters in the hands of Liu-san, and while he was making inquiries I took a stroll through the town, and I had here an opportunity of examining at my leisure the new people in whose country I should be travelling for many hundreds of miles. They formed a strong contrast to the Chinese, and even the Mongols, to whose characteristics I had by this time become accustomed. Less acute, industrious or pushing than the Chinese, and at the same time more intelligent and cultivated than the Mongols, the Turkis struck me as an intelligent though lethargic race. They evidently had no intention of taking life so seriously as their Chinese conquerors, but they possessed sufficiently refined ideas to seek for more material comfort than the easy-going Mongols were disposed to bestir themselves to gain. The Turkis had not energy or virility enough to shake off the Chinese yoke and govern their own country, but they were sufficiently far advanced to build themselves comfortable houses, and to improve their position by trade.

One favourable trait in their character, which

at once struck me coming from China, was their politeness to strangers. In passing through a Chinese town the traveller has always to fear insults from the mob. Here in Hami I could move about if not unnoticed, at any rate unmolested.

It is interesting to note that round Hami was the seat of the Uighurs, the race from whom the Mongols of Chengiz Khan acquired what little learning and cultivation they ever possessed. The men were tall, and some of them really dignified. They were dressed in long coloured cotton robes, and wore on their heads either turbans or small skull caps. The women were very different from the doll-like Chinese women, with painted faces and waddling about on contorted feet; or the sturdy, bustling women of Manchuria; or the simple, silly Mongol girls, with their great red cheeks and dirty unintelligent faces. These Turki women had good features, full round eyes, and complexions not much darker than Greeks or Italians. Dressed in a long loose robe not confined at the waist, with their black tresses of hair allowed to fall over their shoulders in thick plaits, and wearing on their heads a

bright red cap which effectively set off their
prominent features, the appearance of the
Turki women was strikingly picturesque.

Hami I found to be a town of some five or
six thousand inhabitants, with all the bustle of
life customary to a trading centre. There were
fairly good shops and a busy bazaar where men
of many different nationalities met together—
Chinese, Mongols, Kalmacs, Turkis, and others.
Large heavily-laden travelling carts come lum-
bering through the town from Turkestan, and
strings of camels from across the desert. European cotton goods, cloth, native manufactures,
and produce, and all the necessaries of life
were obtainable here. I even bought a bottle
of English sweetmeats.

I was looking out for a shop where it was
said Russian goods could be bought, and, on
finding it, noticed Russian characters above.
I looked behind the counter and was both
surprised and delighted to see a Russian, who
shook hands heartily with me, and asked me
to come inside. He spoke neither Chinese
nor English, but only Russian and Mongol;
and as I could speak neither of those languages
we had to communicate with each other through

a Chinaman, who spoke Mongol. The Russian spoke to him in Mongol and this was translated to me in Chinese, and I replied in Chinese which the Chinaman rendered into Mongol for the benefit of the Russian. This Russian lived in a Chinese house, in Chinese fashion, but was dressed in European clothes. He sold chiefly cotton goods and ironware, such as pails, basins, knives, etc., but trading was not profitable. There had been five Russian merchants here, but two had gone to Kobdo, and two were engaged in hunting down Chinese mandarins to try and get money which was owing to them.

The next evening I invited the Russian round to my inn to dinner. Conversation was difficult, but we managed to spend a very pleasant evening, and drank to the health of our respective sovereigns. I held up my glass and said " Czar," and we drank together. Then I held it up again and said " Skobeleff," and so on through every Russian I had ever heard of. My guest, I am sorry to say, knew very few Englishmen, but he had grasped the fact that we had a Queen, so at five-minute intervals he would drink to her Majesty.

Three years later, when I was at Kashgar, I heard that two Russian merchants residing at Hami had been imprisoned by the Chinese authorities, and treated in the most terrible manner. A European in the employ of the Chinese heard of this, brought it to the notice of the Russian Minister at Peking, and I believe their release was obtained, but not before they had undergone the most fearful sufferings from hunger and imprisonment in foul, pest-stricken dungeons. I have often wondered whether my hearty, good-natured guest was one of them.

Besides the native town of Hami there is also a Chinese walled town, about six hundred yards square, with four gateways, each surmounted by a massive tower; and I subsequently found in travelling through the country that it is the unvarying custom to have the open native town and the Chinese walled town close beside. Every town in Turkestan is therefore double.

We halted four days at Hami, and made a new start for Kashgar—the second great stage of the journey—on July 8. It appeared that carts could be taken the whole way, so the slow

wearisome camels were no longer required. I
was fortunate in being able to effect an excellent arrangement with my "boy" Liu-san,
by which he engaged to land me at Kashgar
by contract on a certain date. I was to be
regarded as a piece of merchandise to be carted
from one place to the other, and he was to
undertake the whole of the arrangement. He
was to land me and my baggage at Kashgar
in forty days, and was to be paid seventy taels
(about £17 10s.) here at Hami, and thirty
taels more if we reached Kashgar in the stipulated time. He was to receive two taels extra
for every day in advance of that time, and two
taels would be deducted for every day more
than the forty days. This arrangement fully
answered my expectations. The money which
was to be made for transport went into my
"boy's," and not into some outsider's pocket,
so that he at once became directly interested
in the journey. And instead of having to go
through all the irritating and irksome process
of perpetually nagging at the servants and
pony-men, which utterly destroys the charm of
travel, I could go about with my mind at rest,
well-assured that my "boy" would be worrying

at me to get up early in the morning, to make
no delay at starting, and to go on for another
few miles instead of halting at a tempting place
in the evening. I became an impassive log,
and enjoyed myself immensely. It was quite
a new sensation to be able to lie lazily on in
bed while breakfast was being got ready; at
the end of breakfast to find everything prepared for the start; and all the way through
to have an enthusiastic and energetic servant
constantly urging me to go on farther and
quicker.

The "boy," with the advance he had received from me, bought up a cart and four
animals (two mules and two ponies), and this
carried all the baggage and supplies of the
party, while I rode a pony. The cart was of
he description known in Turkestan as an
araba, a large covered cart, with only one pair
of very high wheels. One animal was in the
shafts, and three tandem fashion in front. The
weight of the baggage, supplies, etc. (including
a certain amount of grain for the animals),
which the cart carried, was one thousand five
hundred catties (two thousand pounds).

I will not weary my readers with a descrip-

tion of my journey from Hami to Kashgar
stage by stage. Each was very like the other
with but little variation. At distances varying
from ten to twenty miles a small village on an
oasis would be met with, but all between was
barren gravel desert. Away on the right rose
the Tian-shan Mountains, but they were quite
bare and no snowy peaks were visible from the
road. To the left the desert extended without
limit.

The villages were generally small and the
number of ruined houses, betokening the strug-
gles which had lasted many years, was always
noticeable. Small dirty inns, usually kept by
Turkis, were to be found at each stage, but
the accommodation provided was not inviting,
and in preference I used as a rule to sleep on
a mattrass stretched out inside the waggon,
while my meals would be cooked by the side.
The weather was hot, the maximum ranging
from 90° to 98° in the shade, but the air was
dry and healthy, the nights cool, the thermometer falling to about 64°. Occasionally we
experienced a cooling thunderstorm which
freshened the air and laid the dust for a
time.

Altogether the eastern end of Turkestan bore a depressing look.   For every inhabited house we saw we would pass at least two in ruins. In passing through the villages scarcely an inhabitant would be met with, and few were seen working in the fields, and much land which had formerly been cultivated was now lying fallow.   There seemed to be as many Chinese as Turkis, but the Chinese were mostly Mohammedans and in physique inferior to those of China proper.   Little traffic was met with on the road as the summer is not considered a favourable season for travelling.   But occasionally we passed a detachment of soldiers, or a waggon, or strings of donkeys, the principal pack animal of the country, carrying country produce to market.   Grapes are largely grown in this part, dried to raisins, and taken to Hami.

We pushed on rapidly, travelling indifferently day or night, according to the length of the stage, merely halting at the end of each a sufficient length of time to rest the animals, and then starting again, sometimes at eleven o'clock at night, sometimes at four in the morning, and sometimes at two in the afternoon. And now having no tent to pitch and strike, no pack animals to load and unload, and standing in no need of house accommodation, we had nothing to delay us, and covered long stages every day. On one day we accomplished nearly seventy miles, resting only five and a quarter hours in the twenty-four.

Near Pi-chan we passed through a pretty, well-cultivated country, through which ran a charming little stream, its banks lined with graceful poplars and willows. Numerous little irrigation ducts were carried through the fields and straight across the road, rather to the hindrance of traffic; though I found it a real pleasure to hear the cart splashing through water. There were a number of little hamlets dotted over the plain, and many mosques, all built of mud like everything else in the country. Many of them had piles of *Ovis argali* and ibex horns on the ledges of the roofs, but I saw no *Ovis argali* as fine as those which I obtained in the Gobi. At two and a half miles from Pi-chan the delightful oasis came to an end abruptly, and we were on the same dreary old gravel desert again. From a piece of rising ground I obtained a good view of the country we had been passing through. It was very beautiful. The plain, some six miles in length from east to west, and three or four from north to south, was covered over with trees, beneath the shade of which nestled the little Turki hamlets. About a mile to the south of Pi-chan was a remarkable range of sandhills like that I saw in the Gobi, and certainly two or three hundred feet in height.

The afternoon was terribly hot on the gravelly desert, and, after passing over it for sixteen miles, we were glad enough to come upon another oasis, and halt at a pretty village built on the steep bank of a little stream. There was a bustling landlord at the inn, who came out to meet us, and attended to us more in the Manchurian innkeeper style than in the usual listless way they have here. But how different these mud-hovels here called inns were to the well-built hostelries of Manchuria! In the one country timber was abundant, in the other, precious and difficult to obtain, and so nowhere in Chinese Turkestan did I see the well-built inns and farmhouses so characteristic of Manchuria.

We reached Turfan on July 17. As I

passed through the street there was a murmur
of "Oroos," "Oroos," and a small crowd of
Turkis and Chinese collected in the inn yard to
see me. My boy was told there was a Russian
shop in the Turk city, so I immediately went
over there hoping to meet some Europeans.
We dismounted at a shop, and I was received
by a fine-looking Turki who shook hands
and spoke to me in Russian. He then took
me through a courtyard to another courtyard
with a roof of matting. On the ground were
spread some fine carpets, on which sat some
fair-looking men in Turk dress. But I was
disappointed to notice that none of them looked
quite like Russians. They spoke no language
that I knew, and matters were rather at a
standstill, when I heard the word "Hindustani."
I said at once, "Hindustani zaban bol sakta"
("I can speak Hindustani"), and they sent off
for a man who could speak that language.
When he appeared, I had a long talk with him.
He was an Afghan merchant, he said, and he
explained that the men of this house were
Andijani merchants from Russian Turkestan,
and were therefore called Russians. He had
travelled through a great part of India, and

knew Bombay, Calcutta, Delhi, Lahore, and all
the cities of the Punjab.

He asked me if Peking was as big a town as
Calcutta, and was much struck when I told him
the latter was the larger, repeating what I said
to the Andijanis. Peking is so distant that
these Central Asian merchants never visit it,
and the only accounts they have of it are from
the Chinese, who exaggerate to any extent the
greatness of the capital of China and of its
emperor.

The Andijanis were tall, handsome-looking
men, dressed in loose robes of cotton print, and
wearing long black leather boots with high
heels—exactly the same as the Cossacks wear,
but with the bottom part detached from the
upper. This bottom part was a slipper which
they kicked off before stepping on to the carpet,
leaving the long boot still on, but with a soft,
flexible foot.

After tea I again went to the Turk city to
look at the shops. The chief—in fact, almost
the only—articles sold here were cotton fabrics,
principally chintz. Some of them were remarkably pretty, with patterns of flowers, and others
handkerchiefs of many colours, arranged to-

gether in patterns very tastefully. They were
all of European manufacture, some had come
from India, but most from Russia.

While walking through the bazaar I saw a
man with a sharper, keener look than the
ordinary Turki possesses, and suspecting that
he might come from India I addressed him in
Hindustani. To my delight he understood,
and informed me he was an Arab Hajji from
Mecca, who had travelled through India,
Afghanistan, Persia, Egypt, Turkey, and
Bokhara. On my asking him where he expected to go next he said, " Wherever Fate
may lead me."

Some Turkis seeing us standing talking very
politely asked us to come and sit in their shop
and drink tea. Then we had a long talk
together which was especially gratifying to me,
as for months I had not been able to carry on
a connected conversation with anyone. What
however struck me more than his quaint
description of the various countries he had
travelled through was his manner of addressing
the orderly crowd which had collected round,
and the evident influence he had over them. I
soon realised that I was sitting beside no one

M

more nor less than a Mohammedan Missionary, and I marked with interest the effect he produced upon those around him. Simply dressed, but with a natural dignity in his appearance which instinctively commanded respect; intensely earnest, and with an evident reserve of fiery force behind, this pilgrim from Mohammed's native land could sway the people whither he would. Asiatics are naturally eloquent, and a man like this, who passed his life in discoursing at the mosques, and in exchanging ideas with men of many different countries, and who, moreover, bore with him all the prestige which surrounds a dweller in the Holy City, could make the staring Turkis round him believe and do what he liked. Never, indeed, have I been more impressed with the influence which Mohammedan religious leaders can exercise, and how dangerous that influence may be when exercised by ignorant but zealous apostles.

I thought, too, that I was able to realise in some way how religious systems take birth, and religious leaders arise. All the great religions have arisen in the East and perhaps from men not very dissimilar to this Arab

Hajji. Mohammed himself was not, I daresay, very different either in his appearance or his manner. And I could imagine a man of strong personality and great magnetic influence, and with the fiery zeal of an Eastern race so impressing his ideas upon those about him, as to produce an effect which may carry on for centuries after. Asiatic people live more together than inhabitants of colder regions. They constantly meet with one another. Half their day is spent in talking, and they naturally collect round a man who shows a commanding influence. They hang upon his words and lethargically accept the authority he insidiously exerts upon them. Men like this Arab Hajji exert but a passing influence. Others, like the so-called Mahdi in the Sudan, for years sway hundreds of thousands. Mohammed for twelve centuries has influenced millions of the human race. It is but a question of degree.

I had read in some book that at Turfan it was so hot that people lived in holes underground. I never quite believed it, but to-day I found it was a real fact. Here in the inn yard was a narrow flight of steps leading underground. I went down them, and found a room

M 2

with a kang, and a Chinaman lying on it smoking opium. It was perfectly cool below there, and there was no musty smell, for the soil is extremely dry. The room was well ventilated by means of a hole leading up through the roof.

Turfan and its neighbourhood lies at an extremely low altitude. My barometer here read 29·48. My thermometer was broken, so that I cannot record the temperature, but it may be taken at between 90° and 100°—say 95°. Turfan must be between two and three hundred feet below the level of the sea,* which, considering that it is in the heart of the continent several thousand miles from any sea is a sufficiently remarkable fact.

After leaving Turfan and as we neared Karashar we entered a country thickly covered with trees, like a park, with long coarse grass in tufts, and many small streams, one of which was four feet deep and nearly covered the mules and flooded the bottom of the cart while crossing. The rainfall here must be considerably more than farther east. The soil is sandy and

---

* This depression was also noticed by Colonel Bell before my visit, and its existence has since been confirmed by Russian travellers.

apparently not worth cultivating, as we only passed one small hamlet.

On July 24 we reached Karashar, which, like all towns hereabouts, is surrounded by a mud wall, and the gateways surmounted by the usual pagoda-shaped towers.

We had to make a half-halt here, to dry things which had been wetted in the rivers. I went for a stroll round the place. Outside of the walled city there are two streets running down to the Karashar river, which is rather more than half a mile from the walls. Near the river were some encampments of Kalmaks who were very like Mongols, living in yurts, dressed as other Mongols, and wearing pig-tails, the round coloured caps with a tassel, and long coats. They are easily distinguish-able from both Chinese and Turks. I ques-tioned several people about the different races of this part of Turkestan, and was told that there were three different races—the Kitai (Chinese), Tungani, and Turks, and here at Karashar were a few Kalmaks. The Turks do not appear to be divided into tribes, but are called by the town they belong to. The Chinese call them Chan-teu (turban-wearers).

On leaving Karashar we had to cross the river by ferry at the end of the town. It was about one hundred and fifty yards wide, and three to four feet deep, running through a level country, which would be flooded out if the river rose another couple of feet. The boat, which just held our cart and my two ponies, was poled across by three Kalmaks.

At a hundred yards after leaving the ferry we had to ford a branch of the river, some thirty yards broad, and deep enough in places to wet the inside of the cart again. After this we passed over a swamp, and three times our cart stuck. The first time we were three hours trying to get it out of the mud, and it was not till we had taken everything out of the cart, and engaged some Turks to help shove and pull, that we succeeded in doing so. We then got along all right for a couple of miles, when we stuck again, and a second time had to unload everything. We then got clear of the swamp, but stuck a third time in a deep rut! The animals were so exhausted, that it was impossible to get on that night, as it was one o'clock; and we went off to the house of one of the Turks who was helping us, leaving the boy in the cart.

The Turk showed us into a most comfortable room, made of mud only, but looking clean for all that. A kind of dado of chintz had been arranged round the walls, which brightened up the place. On the kang, piles of felts and bedding were rolled up. There were two fireplaces in the room, but no chimney, the smoke going out through a hole in the roof. All sorts of household utensils were hung round the walls, and some mutton and herbs were hanging from a rafter. Everything was clean and neatly arranged, and there was no smell. It was a far superior room to those which are inhabited by the same class of men in an Indian village. My host bustled about to get some bedding ready for me, and brought me some tea, after which I turned in sharp, as I was very tired.

Early the next morning the cart was got out of the rut. I gave twenty-five cents to each of the five men who had helped us, and presented my host with some tea, sugar, candles, and matches. He was delighted, and salaamed profusely; the old lady of the house bowed

very gracefully to me, too, as the things were
brought into the house.   They insisted upon
my having some tea, and the lady produced a
tray with some bread, and flowers, and I parted
from them very favourably impressed with my
first experience of Turki hospitality.

We travelled on till midday, and then halted
to dry our things, for my clothes-bag was full
of water.   At sunset the mosquitoes came in
swarms; and though we lighted four fires to
smoke them off, it had no effect.   We were to
start at 1 A.M., and I lay down between the
fires, but could not get a wink of sleep, which
was rather hard after having been up till one
the night before.

There is little noteworthy to record of the
journey between Karashar and Kuché the next
town at which we arrived.   The oases were
more frequent and larger than in the country
farther east, but otherwise there was little
difference, and we travelled rapidly on only
anxious to reach the buttress ranges of the
Himalayas in time to be able to cross into
India before winter effectually closed the
passes.

On August 2, we arrived at the Kuché

AN OASIS IN CHINESE TURKESTAN.

Page 168.

oasis, and for three miles passed through a country covered with trees and houses. The road also was lined with trees and houses, even before we reached the actual town. The number of trees was indeed quite noticeable, and I remarked some houses which were actually built on to the trees.

We drove into an inn yard, but found there was no room ; and were told that a batch of soldiers was passing through, so all the inns had closed their doors. The gallant defenders of their country are not held in much esteem by their fellow countrymen. A little diplomacy was therefore necessary. After waiting for half an hour in the cart, we managed to induce the landlord to arrange for a room for me.

Two Afghans, who had lived here for twenty years, visited me. Afghans, at any rate out of their own country, are always worth talking to. In comparison with the docile, domestic Turkis they are much more " men of the world, " and I was always interested in having a conversation with them. These two Afghans told me that they had been in Turkestan in the time of Yakub Beg, the native ruler who had been turned out by the Chinese ten years previously.

They talked of those as good times, and spoke of the conduct of the Chinese as very *zabardast* (oppressive), saying the Turks were like sheep to submit to it.

Kuchê town and district has, probably, sixty thousand inhabitants. There are remains of the walls of the old Turk city south-east of the Chinese, but the greater number of houses and all the shops are outside of this. The shops are small, like those in India, and nothing of native manufacture is sold, excepting sheep-skins, which are a speciality of this place.

After leaving Kuchê the country was still more populated, though the greater part of each march was over bare desert or through barren hills. We would also pass through country watered by numerous streams running down from the mountains, the road lined with trees, and snowy mountains in the background. Wheat, oats, and maize were the chief crops. Reaping was just beginning. A noticeable thing in this part was the absence of local carts. They were not used at all for farm purposes or for carrying country produce into town. Donkeys only were employed for this, and one

only sees a few travelling carts used for long
journeys.

On August 7 we arrived at Aksu, the largest
town we had yet seen. It had a garrison of
two thousand soldiers, and a native population
of about twenty thousand, beside the inhabitants
of the surrounding district. There were large
bazaars and several inns—some for travellers,
others for merchants wishing to make a pro-
longed stay to sell goods. A trader will bring
goods from a distant town, engage a room in
one of these inns or *serais*, and remain there
for some months, or even a year or two, till he
has sold his goods. He will then buy up a
new stock, and start off to another town. It
is in these *serais* that one meets the typical
travelling merchant of Central Asia; and often
have I envied these men their free, independent, wandering life, interspersed with enough
of hardships, of travel, and risks in strange
countries to give it a relish. They are always
interesting to talk to: intelligent, shrewd, full
of information. Naturally they are well-disposed
to Englishmen, on account of the encouragement we give to trade; but they are cos-
mopolitan, and do not really belong to any

country except that in which they are at the time living. And this habit of rubbing up against men of so many different countries gives them a quiet, even temperament and breadth of idea which makes them charming company.

I engaged one of these men, a native of the Pathan state of Bajaur on our Indian frontier, and which I eight years later visited during the Chitral expedition. His name was Rahmat-ula-Khan, and he agreed to accompany me to Kashgar, by Ush Turfan, while my cart went by Maral-bashi. He was a good specimen of his class, and full of adventurous projects, his great ambition being to visit England.

Under the guidance of this man, I left Aksu on August 10, riding one pony myself, while another was ridden by the Turki servant, and a third, carrying all the baggage we took with us, was led. In this way we could travel fast, and make long marches. Several of the cheery sociable merchants from India accompanied us for the first half of the march, and provided a lunch in a garden under the cool shade of fruit trees. The country, for several miles beyond Aksu, was well cultivated, and the road good. We crossed the Aksu river,

divided into many branches, a mile wide in all,
the water in the deep channels being waist-
deep, and the next day arrived at Ush Turfan,
a picturesque little town at the foot of a rugged
hill, with a fort on its summit.

From here we passed through a country
cultivated at first, but afterwards relapsing into
the more or less barren condition which is
characteristic of the district.   The sides of
the hills which bounded the valley we were
ascending were not, however, so utterly barren
as many we had passed.   There was a quantity
of scrub and small bushes on them, and, higher
up, fine grassy slopes in places.   At the end of
the march we reached a Kirghiz encampment
of twenty-two tents.   Here were the first
Kirghiz I had met; but most of the men were
with their flocks and herds, higher up on the
mountain-sides, and it was only the very old
and the very young that were left below with
what might be called the heavy camp equipage.
Having no tent of my own, and there being no
public inn, I was obliged to do as the people
of the country do, and seek the hospitality of
the inhabitants of the tents.   This was, as
usual, readily given.   We rode up to a tent,

and Rahmat-ula-Khan went in, said we were
travelling to Kashgar, and asked for accommodation for the night. In this way I found
myself quartered in a tent with four old ladies,
one of whom was a great-grandmother, and the
youngest a grandmother. But their hospitality
was equal to their age, and we took a mutual
interest in each other. The tent was similar in
construction to the yurts of the Mongols, but
these Kirghiz seemed much better off than any
of the Mongols I had met, or than the Kirghiz
we afterwards saw on the Pamirs. They were
well clothed in long loose robes of stout cotton
cloth—generally striped—of Russian manufacture. Round the tents were piles of clothes
and bedding for the winter—good stout felts
and warm quilts ; and rows of boxes to contain
the household goods and treasures. A small
portion of the tent was always partitioned off,
and there were kept the supplies of milk,
cream, and curds, which form the staple food
of the Kirghiz. On the whole, the tents were
clean and comfortable, and by living *en famille*
with these Kirghiz, I got to see a great deal
more of their customs and habits than I otherwise should have done.

Meanwhile, as I was looking round the tent, my hostesses were examining my kit, and showing the greatest interest in it. I had to take off my boots and socks, and it so happened that my socks had holes. This immediately appealed to the feminine instinct; they were whisked away, and one of the old ladies proceeded carefully to mend them. Good old soul, it quite reminded one of more homelike times to be looked after in this way! After mending the socks, the lady devoutly said her prayers, and was followed by the others one after another, so that throughout the time I was with them one or other of the old ladies always appeared to be praying.

In the evening all the cows, sheep and goats, which had been left in the encampment, were collected and milked, and one or two young kids brought into the tent to be better looked after. The milk was rich in cream, and delicious to drink. But the Kirghiz drink whey mostly, and they have a method of rolling the nearly solidified curds into balls about the size of a man's fist, and drying these balls in the sun to keep for the winter or for a journey. Balls of curds like these are not

very appetising, but they are much consumed
by the Kirghiz. All the bowls for collecting
the milk are of wood, and by no means so
cleanly kept as one would like to see ; I doubt,
in fact, if they are ever thoroughly cleaned.
The milk of one day is poured out, and that
of the next poured in, and so on for month
after month. Still, the milk always seems fresh
and good, and it is one of the luxuries which
form the reward for travelling among the
Kirghiz.

The proprietresses of the tent I was in had
their dinner of curds and milk and a little
bread, and then, as it grew dark, they said it
was time to go to bed. They first said their
prayers, then took down one of the piles of
bedding (bedsteads were, of course, unknown),
and insisted on making up a bed of quilts and
felts for me ; and then, having made up their
own also, and pulled a felt over the hole in
the roof in case it might rain during the night,
took themselves to their beds, and we all slept
comfortably till morning.

On the following day we continued up the
valley, and every few miles passed a small
encampment of Kirghiz. We were, in fact,

regularly in the Kirghiz preserves. These nomads are not cultivators, as a rule, but we passed a few patches of cultivation, and what was very remarkable was that this cultivation was very often—generally indeed in this valley —of poppies. On inquiry, I found that, though the Kirghiz do not smoke opium themselves, they find poppies a most paying crop to grow, and can sell the produce much more profitably than that of any other crop.

Two days later we arrived in what is known as the Syrt country. There was no particular road here, but merely the tracks of animals leading in many directions. We had brought a Kirghiz with us to show the way, but this he now refused to do, and eventually he left us stranded in the midst of a series of bare, low hills and sterile plains, without apparently any water, any inhabitants, or any special road. We knew, too, that what people we should meet had not a good reputation, and were said to rob and even murder travellers, and matters looked unpleasant. We pushed on, however, in the general direction of Kashgar, and towards evening, after a very hard march, reached an encampment of six tents. The

owner of the one we applied to was very surly,
but eventually agreed to give us accommodation
for the night.

It was, therefore, with no very grateful
feelings towards him that we left his camp on
the following morning. We travelled hard all
day, and, at the end of a march of forty-six
miles, over a country mostly composed of bare
hills and gravel plains, but with occasional
clumps of trees in the hollows, we reached a
wide plain of light clay, in the middle of which
we found a large encampment of fully a hundred tents, and the people, besides keeping
large flocks and herds, also cultivated a considerable amount of land.   I noticed, too, some
houses scattered here and there over the cultivated part of the plain, but was told that these
were merely storehouses. The Kirghiz said
that houses were good enough to put stores of
grain in, but they would never run the risk of
living in any erection which might fall down
like a house ! The inhabitants of this encampment were far from friendly, and it was only
after considerable difficulty that a man was
found who was willing to put us up. Rahmat-
ula-Khan was most tactful and persuasive, but

he told me that night that the people were
badly disposed towards us, and advised me to
be watchful.

Next morning matters were worse. As I
mounted to ride away, crowds of these rough
Kirghiz collected round me, gesticulating wildly.
I asked Rahmat-ula-Khan what was the matter,
and he said that they had determined not to
let me through their country. They argued
that no European had been through before
(though this was not true, as a party of British
officers from Sir Douglas Forsyth's Mission
came into their country as far as the Below-ti
Pass), and that they did not see any reason
why I should be allowed to. Some of the
more excited were for resorting to violent
measures, but Rahmat-ula-Khan, who all the
time was keeping very quiet and even smiling,
talked and reasoned with them, while I sat on
my pony and looked on, well knowing that the
Pathan could arrange matters best by himself.

It was curious to watch the gradual effect of
his arguments, and the cool way in which he
proceeded. He first of all drew them out, and
allowed them to expend all the spare energy
for vociferation they possessed, and then asked

them what advantage was to be gained by stopping me. He said I had come direct from Peking, and had a passport from the Emperor of China, which I could show them; and that, having that passport, my whereabouts was known, so that if anything happened to me they would have Chinese soldiers swarming over their country, and every sort of harm done them. He then went on to say that as far as he was concerned it was a matter of indifference whether they let me through or not; but, looking at the question from an outside point of view, it certainly seemed to him wiser on their part to let me go quietly on to the next place, and so end the matter. If they acted thus, nothing more would be heard of me; whereas, if they did anything to me, a good deal more might come of it. The upshot of the affair was that they allowed themselves to be persuaded, and it was agreed that I should be permitted to proceed on my way. Rahmat-ula-Khan had successfully extracted me from what might have been a very awkward situation.

He was one of the best men for this kind of work I could have found, for he was always

well-spoken with the people, and cool in difficulties. He was a good companion, too, and
on the long marches and in the evenings in the
tent, he used to tell me of his travels, in the
course of which he had been in Egypt, and
was in Constantinople at the time of the
Russian war. What struck him most about
the Russians was that their soldiers were
" pukka," that is, hardy. They were not so
well treated as ours in the way of food and
clothing, but they were " pukka," he kept on
repeating, and ready to go through any amount
of hardships. The trait he did not like in the
Russians was their passion for passports ; they
were always at him for his passport, so that
there was always a certain amount of difficulty
or obstruction in moving about, and this inter-
fered with his constitutional habit of roving.
He was a strict Mohammedan, and seemed to
me to be always praying, though he assured
me he only did so the regulation five times a
day. As to us, he thought we had no religion.
He had observed us going to church on Sun-
days, but that was only once a week, and he
did not know what we did for the remainder of
the seven days.

We determined now to march on as hard as
we could till we got out of the country inhabited by Kirghiz, and down into the plains
again, where the people were all Turkis.   This
we succeeded in doing the same day.   We
followed down a stream, and then, after passing
a small Chinese post, emerged on to the great
plain of Turkestan again near Artysh.

From here I saw one of those sights which
almost strike one dumb at first—a line of snowy
peaks apparently suspended in mid-air.   They
were the Pamir Mountains, but they were so
distant, and the lower atmosphere was so laden
with dust, that their base was hidden, and only
their snowy summits were visible.   One of these
was over twenty-five thousand feet high, and
another twenty-two thousand, while the spot
where I stood was only four thousand ; so their
height appeared enormous and greater still on
account of this wonderful appearance of being
separated from earth.

Here, indeed, was a landmark of progress.
More than a thousand miles back I had first
sighted the end of the Tian-shan Mountains
from the desert.   I had surmounted their
terminal spurs, and then travelled week after

week for nearly a thousand miles along their base, their summits constantly appearing away on my right hand. Now at last arose in front of me the barrier which was to mark the point where I should turn off left and south to India. It was a worthy termination of that vast plain, for the greater part desert, which stretches for four thousand miles from the borders of Man-·churia to the buttress range of the Pamir, both extremities of which I had now visited.

That evening we reached Artysh. Every-thing here looked thriving and prosperous. The fruit season was at its height, and all along the road, at any little garden, the most delicious grapes and melons could be obtained. Nor was there now any difficulty with the people, and they were always ready to allow us to rest for a time in their gardens or put us up for the night.

We now emerged on to the Kashgar plain, passed through a populous, well-cultivated district covered with trees and fruit gardens, and at length entered the town of Kashgar, the distance to which, when I was starting from Peking, had seemed so vast. Here I was at last, and the culminating point of my journey had been reached. For the rest of the way I should be, so to speak, on my return. Kashgar was well known, too, from the Indian side, and there was a Russian consul stationed there. So when I reached the place I appeared to have arrived again on the fringes of civilisation.

Passing through the native town, we put up at an inn on the southern side. I sent my card and passport to the yamen, and very shortly afterwards the Afghan Aksakal and a number of Indian traders came to see me. These Aksakals are men selected by the Chinese from among the traders of each country as their representatives. They are responsible for reporting any new arrivals, and all dealings with their countrymen are carried on by the Chinese through them. They correspond to a certain extent to consuls, and perform some of the functions of a consul, but they are appointed and removed at the pleasure of the Chinese. This Afghan Aksakal, though he was afterwards suspected of having sheltered the murderer of Mr. Dalgleish (to whom I will refer presently), and had to leave Kashgar, made himself most useful, and greatly impressed me.

KASHGAR.

Page 184.

He struck me as a born soldier: strong-willed,
capable, and made to command. He and
many of the traders of the place—Afghans,
Peshawuris, Badakhshis, and others—were with
me nearly the whole day long during my few
days' stay in Kashgar. Tea and fruit were
always ready, and they used to sit round and
talk. The Afghan's conversation was mostly
of fighting, and of rifles and revolvers. Every
kind of firearm he seemed to know, and to have
his own opinion about it as to its efficiency.
The Russian Berdan rifle he preferred to our
Martini, and he thought the Americans made
better revolvers than we did. At the time the
Chinese re-took Kashgar he was in the town,
and said there was practically no fighting.
Yakub Beg had died, or been poisoned,
away westward some weeks before, and he
being dead, there was no one to lead the
defence, and the people of the country were
absolutely apathetic. What soldiers there were,
when they heard the Chinese were close to the
town, hastily threw aside their uniforms or
disguises as soldiers, and, assuming the dress of
cultivators, walked about the fields in a lamb-
like and innocent manner. The Chinese en-

tered the town, and everything went on as if
nothing had happened—the shopkeeper sold his
wares, and the countryman ploughed his fields,
totally indifferent as to who was or who was
not in power in Kashgar. Only the ruling
classes were affected, and most of them had
fled.

The Afghan merchants would often talk, too,
of our last war with them. Some of them had
fought against us. They asked me one day
where " Ropert " was. I did not quite understand at first who or what they meant. But
they explained that he (it was a person apparently) was a first rate man to fight, and then
it struck me that they meant General Roberts.
They had a great admiration for him. One of
them said that he had set out from Kandahar
to Kabul, but on the way had " met " General
Roberts, and had returned. I was told afterwards that he had been in three fights with the
British, but here, outside his own country, he
was friendly enough with an Englishman, and
he said he admired us for being able to fight
quite as well as Afghans ! They have a rather
overpowering pride at times, these Afghans;
but, on the whole, one likes them for their

manliness. They are *men*, and at any rate, they are very good fellows to meet and talk with as one could do in a Kashgar *serai*. It was noticeable, too, that they never lost their respect either for themselves or for the Englishman they were talking with, so that we could converse perfectly freely and openly. Altogether I much enjoyed my talk with them.

I was rather out of sorts the day after my arrival, but on the second I went to call on the Russian consul. The Afghan Aksakal had an idea that Russians and Englishmen were like cats and dogs in their relation towards each other, and that they could not meet without fighting. So, just as I was mounting my pony to go off, he caught me by the arm and whispered confidentially to me, " Now, sahib, do your best to be polite, and don't go fighting with that Russian." I found M. Petrovsky, the Russian consul, living in a native house, which, by improvements, he had made very comfortable. He and his secretary, M. Lutsch, received me most cordially, and sent for a missionary, M. Hendriks, who lived close by, to come and see me and hear the account of my journey from Peking. The talk turned on India, and I was astonished to find how well acquainted M. Petrovsky was with that country. He showed me with pride many volumes by the best English writers on Indian subjects, and the most recent parliamentary Blue Books on the country. The annual parliamentary report on the " Material and Moral Progress of India " was one which he took in regularly, and admired much. He had known the present Amir of Afghanistan, Abdul Rahman, at the time he was a refugee in Samarcand, and he knew the names and a good deal of the personal history of most of the leading men in Kashmir. On the Central Asian question he spoke very freely, and said that we English always suspected the Russians of designs upon India, but that in reality nothing was further from their minds.

When I returned to the *serai* from my visit to the consul, the Afghan Aksakal eyed me closely, to see if there were any signs of a scrimmage with the Russian, and when I told him that M. Petrovsky was coming on the following morning to return my visit, he seemed relieved. I said I should want the room I was occupying made respectable to receive him in, and he immediately darted off in his usual impetuous manner, saying he would arrange everything. Shortly afterwards good carpets, chairs, a table, teapot, cups, saucers, and plates, came pouring in, and the room was in a few moments transformed into a civilised abode.

On the following morning the consul, with an escort of sixteen mounted Cossacks and the Russian flag, rode into the *serai*. We had another long conversation together, and I found it a great pleasure to talk again with a European, after so many months of travel. M. Petrovsky is an especially interesting man to talk with, and I was sorry I could not stay longer in Kashgar to see more of him.

But, Liu-san having arrived with the cart, I had to start off again for Yarkand. Liu-san had fulfilled his contract, and landed everything in Kashgar exactly in the time stipulated— forty days from Hami—a good performance, with which I was very much pleased. Between Kashgar and Yarkand there was nothing of special interest that had not been noted by previous travellers. We had made the turn southwards, and now the Pamir Mountains, instead of being straight in front of us, were passed by on our right hand.

On August 29 we reached Yarkand, and were met outside by the Kashmir Aksakal and a large number of Indian traders, who had heard that an English officer was coming to Yarkand, and had come out to meet me. An Englishman always receives a warm welcome from natives of India in foreign countries. I have been told that it is all because of self-interest, and that they merely do it because they hope to get something out of him. Possibly this may be so, but I prefer to think that there is also some tinge of warmth of heart in it, and a feeling of kinship with their rulers which attracts them in a strange land to an Englishman. At any rate, that was the impression produced upon me by my reception in Yarkand, and I would rather retain that than make way for the colder reasoning which had been suggested to me.

In the best Chinese inn in the place the chief room had been made ready for me by the Kashmir Aksakal. Carpets, chairs, and tables from his own house had been brought in, and large plates and baskets piled with fruit—presents from the merchants—came pouring in. Everything was done to make me comfortable, and the feeling that I was nearing my destination increased.

CHAPTER VIII.

INTO THE HEART OF THE HIMALAYAS.

YARKAND was the last town of Chinese Turkestan I visited, and now that I had traversed
the entire length of the country, a brief general
description of it may be interesting. The chief
characteristic of its physical features is undoubtedly the amount of desert comprised in it.
The whole country is, in fact, nothing but a
desert, with patches of cultivation along the
streams which flow down from the mountains,
showing out sharp and distinct like green
splotches on a sepia picture. On three sides
this desert is shut in by ranges of snowy mountains very like the letter U, and on the fourth
side it stretches away uninterruptedly for nearly
two thousand miles. The mountain slopes are
as bare as the plains, and were it not for the
oases, no more inhospitable country could be
imagined. But these oases are what save it.

Once out of the surrounding desert, the traveller finds himself amidst the most inviting
surroundings—cool shady lanes with water-
courses running in every direction, alongside
the road, across it, and under it, giving life
to everything where before all was dead and
bare and burnt.   On either hand, as far as
can be seen, lie field after field of ripening
crops, only broken by the fruit gardens and
shady little hamlets.   Everything seems in
plenty.   Fruit is brought before you in huge
trayfuls, and wheat is cheaper than even in
India.

In this way it is a land of extremes.   On
one side nothing—not the possibility of anything; on the other—plenty.   And the climate
has as great extremes as the physical appearance.   The summer is scorchingly hot anywhere outside the small portion that is cultivated and shaded with trees; and in the winter
the thermometer falls to zero Fahrenheit.
This is the natural result of the position of the
country in the very heart of the greatest continent, where none of the tempering effects of
the sea could possibly reach it.

The people, however, do not share this

o

characteristic of running to extremes. They are the essence of imperturbable mediocrity. They live in a land where—in the places in which anything at all can be grown—the necessaries of life can be produced easily and plentifully. Their mountain barriers shield them from severe outside competition, and they lead a careless, easy, apathetic existence. Nothing disturbs them. Revolutions have occurred, but they have mostly been carried out by foreigners. One set of rulers has suddenly replaced another set, but the rulers in both instances have nearly all been foreigners. Yakub Beg was a foreigner, and most of the officials under him were foreigners, so that even when their hereditary rulers—the Chinese —were driven out for a time, the people of Chinese Turkestan did not govern themselves. On the contrary, in all these changes, they appear to have looked on with indifference. Such a people are, as might naturally be inferred, not a fighting race. They are a race of cultivators and small shopkeepers, and nothing more, and nothing would make them anything more. It is their destiny, shut away here from the rest of the world, to lead a dull, spiritless, but easy and perhaps happy life, which they allow nothing to disturb.

How different all this is to what we had found in Manchuria! There we had the keen, industrious Chinaman, working his very hardest —working away rom morning to night, not to live merely, but to get the utmost he could out of the land, accumulating his wealth, seeking your custom, doing all he could to improve his position. The ruins, the dilapidated towns of Turkestan, were practically unknown there, and the large concentrated villages, instead of farmhouses scattered, as in Turkestan, indifferently over the country, or situated among the fields of the owner, spoke of a people among whom the sterner habits of brigandage were known. Of the two races, the Chinese were evidently born to have the upper hand; but whether they therefore enjoy life so thoroughly as the easy-going Turki is a question open to doubt.

Yarkand, as I have said, was the last town in Turkestan I should pass through, and here I had to make preparations for the journey across the Himalayas. On entering the town I received a letter from Colonel Bell, written on the Karakoram Pass, saying he had just heard of my being in Chinese Turkestan, and telling me, instead of following him along the well-known and extremely barren and uninteresting route by Leh to India, to try the unexplored but direct road by the Mustagh Pass on Baltistan and Kashmir. This was a suggestion which delighted me. It was something quite new, and promised to be difficult enough to be really worth doing. I therefore set to with my preparations for it with a will.

The first thing, of course, was to get guides. Fortunately, there are a large number of Baltis —about two thousand—settled in the Yarkand district, and the Kashmir Aksakal said he would easily be able to obtain men for me. Then ponies had to be collected. Here, too, there was no difficulty, for Yarkand abounds in ponies, and I used to examine thirty or forty a day. Sheepskin coats for the men, supplies for the road, shoes for the ponies, etc., could also be easily procured. So, having set one or two of the merchants to work at these preparations, I took a look round Yarkand.

Hitherto, since leaving Peking, I had purposely kept from visiting the Chinese officials, partly because I had no proper interpreter, and partly because I was travelling in such a quiet way that the official probably would not care to return my visit in a wretched traveller's inn. Chinese officials surround themselves with a good deal of state when they appear in public, and it seems to go as much against the grain with them to visit a stray foreigner in a traveller's *serai* as it would to the mayor of an English town if he were expected to get into his full livery and go with all civic ceremony to call upon a wandering Chinaman putting up at the local " Blue Posts." As a rule, therefore, I merely sent my passport and my card up to the chief official, said I had just arrived, and would leave the next day, or whenever it was, and that I regretted I should not be able to do myself the pleasure of calling on him. But this governor of Yarkand showed particular civility, and sent me several friendly messages, so I called upon him on the afternoon after my arrival.

He received me with the usual politeness of a Chinese official, but with more cordiality. His residence here in Yarkand, at the very extremity of the Chinese Empire, was of

precisely the same pattern and character as
those in Peking itself, and his official dress was
exactly similar to that of any official in the
heart of China.   In whatever part of the
Chinese Empire you visit an official, you
will always find both his residence and his
official dress precisely the same : the loose
blue silk jacket and petticoat, and either the
mushroom hat in summer, or the pork-pie hat
in winter.   No change or variation, whether
the office is civil or military.   Difference in
rank is shown only by a slightly increased
amount of gold for the higher grades on the
square plate of embroidery in the centre of the
jacket, and by the colour of the button on the
top of the hat.

The Governor of Yarkand received me in
one of his private rooms, and we had a long
conversation together.   He had never been to
Peking, and asked many questions about it, and
about the road by which I had come, which he
said no Chinese officials ever thought of using.
An hour after I had reached the inn again, he
came to make a return call upon me, and in
every way showed a friendly feeling.   This
Amban was one of the best governors Yarkand

has had, and, contrary to the usual custom of the Chinese officials, he had taken considerable pains to construct canals for the extension of cultivation, and to build new bazaars in the city.

Yarkand is the largest town I had seen in Turkestan. There are, as everywhere in this country, two towns, the native and the Chinese, but at Yarkand these are connected by a bazaar a few hundred yards in length. The latter is almost entirely new, but the native town is old and dilapidated. The houses are built of mud, as a rule, and there are no very striking buildings to arrest one's interest. All the streets have that dusty, dirty, uncared-for appearance so characteristic of Central Asian towns, and outside the bazaars there is little life. Yarkand, however, is the centre of a considerable trade, and in the autumn large caravans start for and arrive from India at frequent intervals, and the bazaars are then crowded.

A number of the merchants engaged in this trade gave me one day a sumptuous feast in a fruit garden a short distance outside Yarkand. Few people better know the way to enjoy life and make themselves comfortable than these merchants. We first of all sat about under the shade of the trees, while huge bunches of grapes and delicious melons and peaches were freshly plucked and brought to us to eat. Then dinner was announced, and after water for washing the hands had been passed round, we set to at dish after dish of "pillaos" and stews, all beautifully cooked, and we ended up with a pudding which it would be hard to beat anywhere, made of whipped egg, sugar, and other ingredients. All the time the merchants were chaffing away amongst themselves, and were as "gay" and talkative as Frenchmen. One could scarcely wish for better company or more genial hosts. On the way home we had races, each merchant trying to make out that his own horse was better than the others These men are a curious mixture of Eastern gravity and politeness, and boyish spirits and fun. They will come to call on you, and talk away with the greatest solemnity and deference. You meet them next day out for a burst of enjoyment, and every sign of gravity is thrown away, and they are as free and natural and full of life as children.

With the aid of a committee of some of these, my preparations for the attack of the Mustagh Pass progressed most favourably. The services of a first-rate guide were secured ; his name was Wali, and he was a native of Askole, the nearest village on the Kashmir side of the pass. It was many years since he had come to Yarkand by the route, but he undertook to say he had not forgotten it, and could guide me by it all right. Besides him, three other Baltis were enlisted to carry loads, if it should be found impossible to take ponies over the pass. Thirteen ponies were bought, and four Ladakis engaged to look after them. Among these Ladakis was a man named Mohamed Esa (formerly Drogpa), who had accompanied Messrs. Carey and Dalgleish to Tibet, and whom Colonel Bell had sent back to me to help me through. He was placed in charge of the caravan, and made responsible for its efficiency. Three complete sets of shoes for each pony were taken, and new pack-saddles and blankets. All the men were thoroughly well equipped with heavy sheepskin coats, fur caps, and new footgear. Orders were sent on to Kugiar, the last principal village on the

Yarkand side, to have three weeks' supplies for men and ponies ready there, and these supplies for the men included rice, *ghi* (clarified butter), tea, sugar, and some sheep to drive along with us, so that the men should be fit and work willingly; for, after all, the success of the enterprise would depend upon them, not upon me, and all I could do was to see that nothing which foresight could provide for should be left undone before the start was made. Lastly, we took some good strong ropes and a pickaxe or two, to help us over the ice and bad ground.

All these preparations having been completed, we left Yarkand on September 8. The next day we reached the thriving little town of Kargalik. It was market day, and all the roads were crowded with country people coming in to sell their produce, and buy any necessaries for the week. I have not mentioned these market days before, but they are a regular institution in Turkestan. Each town and village fixes a day in the week for its market day, and on that day the bazaars are crowded with people, and it is then that the country people do all their business. In small places the bazaar is absolutely empty all the

A BAZAAR IN CHINESE TURKESTAN.

Page 202.

rest of the week ; the shops are there, but their
doors are shut.   Then on the market day
everything bursts into life, and hundreds of
men and women from the country round, all
dressed in their best, come swarming in.

We put up that day in a delightful fruit
garden, and my bed was made in a bower of
vines, where the grapes hung in enormous
clusters, ready to drop into my mouth.   Two
days later we reached Kugiar, an extensive
village, where all supplies were gathered, in
preparation for our plunge into the mountains.
We were now among the outlying spurs of the
great barrier which divides the plains of India
from those of Turkestan.   Of this barrier the
nearest range is called the Kuen-lun, the centre
the Mustagh or Karakoram, and the farthest
the Himalayas.

On leaving Kugiar we headed directly into
these mountains, and were fairly launched on
our voyage of exploration, though the first
three marches had been traversed by members
of the Forsyth Mission.   We crossed an easy
pass named the Tupa Dawan, and then ascended
a valley in which were a few huts and some felt
tents belonging to a race called Pakhpu.

Leaving this valley, I crossed the Chiragh-saldi Pass, over the main ridge of the Kuen-lun Mountains. The only aneroid I had was un-fortunately not made to register up to such heights as the pass, but I computed its height at about sixteen thousand feet. We were now getting into the heart of our work, and as I looked out from the summit of that pass on to the labyrinth of pathless mountains, rising into tier after tier of snowy peaks, I felt that there was some real stern work before us, and that each one of our little party would have to brace himself up to do his very best if we wished to accomplish the task that had been set us. There were now no paths and no inhabitants. We were alone among the mountains, and it was not only the difficulties which they might present that we had to contend against; we also had to be ever-watchful against an attack from the Kanjuti robbers, who had for many years infested these parts, issuing from their strongholds in Hunza, raiding on caravans trading between Yarkand and Leh by the Karakoram route, and even levying blackmail from villages in the Kugiar district. Three of the men I had with me had actually been cap-

tured by these robbers and afterwards sold into
slavery.   It was necessary to take every pre-
caution; and, as it is their habit to attack at
night, cut the ropes of the tent and let it down
on the top of you, if you are unwary enough to
use one, we had to live in the open, even on
the glaciers, and, however cold it might be,
sheltering ourselves behind any friendly rock
we could find, and after dark always altering
the position we had ostentatiously assumed
during daylight, so that if any Kanjutis happened to have been watching us then, they
might be unable to find us.

Descending from the Chiraghsaldi Pass, we
followed down the pebbly bed of a stream.
But soon the stream disappeared under the
stones, nor could we find grass or bushes for
fuel, and the three great requisites of a traveller,
water, wood, and grass, were all missing.   Darkness came on, and with it a snowstorm; but
still we plodded on, as under these circumstances there was no possibility of encamping.
Stumbling along over the heavy boulders, we at
last came across some bushes, and a little farther
on the stream appeared again; grass was found
on its edges, and we encamped for the night.

On the following day we reached the Yarkand River at Chiraghsaldi camping-ground—
the farthest point reached by Hayward on his
march down the river nearly twenty years
before. The river was at this time of the
year fordable, and ran over a level pebbly bed,
the width of the valley at the bottom being
three or four hundred yards. All along the
bottom were patches of jungle, and here and
there stretches of grass; but the mountain-sides
were quite bare.

Proceeding down the Yarkand River, now
through absolutely unknown country, we reached
the next day the ruins of half a dozen huts and
a smelting furnace, on a plain called Karash-
tarim. There were also signs of furrows, as of
land formerly cultivated, and it is well known
that up to a comparatively recent period, certainly within eighty years ago, this valley of
the Yarkand River was inhabited, and spots
like this, which included about a hundred and
fifty acres of arable land, were cultivated. The
district is known as Raskam, which, I was told,
is a corruption of Rást-kán (a true mine), a
name which was probably given it on account
of the existence of mineral deposits there.

Both on this journey and another which I made down this valley in 1889 I found the remains of old smelting furnaces in several places, and was informed that copper was the mineral extracted.   In the Bazardarra valley, on the right bank of the Yarkand River, there are said to be traces of gold.   The Kanjuti raids were the cause of the country becoming depopulated, and now that these have been effectually stopped by the British Government we may expect to see Raskam in future years again spring into life.

One march below Karash-tarim the valley narrowed considerably, and high cliffs constantly approached the river, making it necessary for us to cross and recross it frequently. At length the stream became confined in a gorge, called the Khoja Mohamed gorge, and was here shut in between cliffs of enormous height and nearly perpendicular.   Through this gorge the river rushed with tremendous force, and, as it was quite unfordable, we were brought to a standstill.   We unloaded the ponies, and every man of us set to work to make a road round the base of the cliff by throwing rocks and boulders into the river, and so building up a way. By the next morning we had succeeded in making a narrow pathway round the cliff. The loads were first carried over this; then the ponies were carefully led along, till at last the whole party was safely conveyed to the other side of this formidable obstacle.

A short distance below, on the left bank of the Yarkand River, we struck a tributary named the Surakwat, up which led the route to the Mustagh Pass, so we here left the valley of the Yarkand River. For a few hundred yards above the junction the Surakwat flows through a very narrow gorge, which the stream fills up completely, and through this gorge the guide now led us, though I found, in 1889, that a much better road led over the top. The boulders over which the torrent dashed were covered with ice, and it was cruel work taking the ponies up. They were constantly slipping and falling back, cutting their hocks and knees to pieces. But we got them through without accident, and emerged on to a wide plain, evidently the bed of a lake, which must have been formed by the rocky obstacle we had passed through before the stream had cut its way down to its present level and thus afforded an outlet to the dammed-up waters.

This plain, which was covered with jungle of dwarf birch and willow or poplar, extended for about two miles. At a couple of miles from the gorge, and again at about nine miles, considerable streams flow in on the right bank of the Surakwat, and, at a mile from the last, two more narrow gorges were passed through ; though here again, on my journey up here in 1889, we succeeded in making a road round to circumvent them. It was altogether a bad day's march for both men and ponies, but at last, toward evening, we found the valley opening to a wide plain, with plenty of scrub on it, where we encamped for the night. Before us rose a great wall of snowy mountains, with not the very smallest sign of a pass, though the guide said we should have to cross them on the following day. I felt some misgivings on looking at this barrier which now stopped our way, for the guide frankly confessed that he had forgotten the way across, and of course there was no sign of a path to guide us. He said, however, that possibly, as we got nearer, he might remember which

P

turning we should have to take, and with that amount of consolation we had to settle down for the night.

We now had our first taste of real cold. We were about fifteen thousand feet above the sea-level, and as soon as the sun set one could almost *see* the cold stealing over the mountains—a cold grey crept over them, the running streams became coated with ice, and as soon as we had had our dinner—we always dined together, to save trouble and time in cooking—and darkness had fairly fallen, we took up our beddings from the places where we had ostentatiously laid them out to mislead any prowling Kanjutis, and hurried off to deposit them behind any rock which would shelter us from the icy wind which blew down from the mountains. It is a curious fact, but when real difficulties seem to be closing around, one's spirits rise. As long as you have health—that is the main point to look after, but it is easily attained in mountain travel—and provided that you take plenty of food, difficulties seem only to make you more and more cheery. Instead of depressing you, they only serve to brace up all your faculties to their highest pitch; and though, as I lay down that night, I felt that for the next two or three weeks we should have harder and harder work before us, I recollect that evening as one of those in all my life in which I have felt in the keenest spirits.

At the first dawn of day on the following morning we were astir. The small stream was frozen solid, and the air bitingly cold ; so we hurried about loading up, to keep ourselves warm, had a good breakfast, and, as the sun rose, started off straight at the mountain wall —a regular battlement of rocky peaks covered with snow, where it was possible, but for the most part too steep for snow to lie. After travelling for three or four miles, a valley suddenly opened up to the left. The guide immediately remembered it, and said that up it was an easy pass which would completely outflank the mountain barrier. The going was good. I left the ponies, and in my eagerness hurried on rapidly in front of them, straining to see the top of the pass, and the "other side "—that will-o'-the-wisp which ever attracts explorers and never satisfies them, for there is ever another side beyond. The height was beginning to tell, and the pass seemed to

P 2

recede the nearer I approached it. One rise after another I surmounted, thinking it would prove the summit. The valley was wide and open, and the going perfectly easy, leading sometimes over round boulders, but more often loose soil. At length I reached a small lake, about a quarter of a mile in length, and a small rise above it at the farther end was the last one of all and the summit of the pass was reached. I rushed up, and there before me lay the "other side," and surely no view which man has ever seen can excel that. To describe the scene in words would be impossible. There are no words with which to do so, and to attempt it with those that are at our disposal would but stain its simple grandeur and magnificence.

Before me rose tier after tier of stately mountains, among the highest in the world— peaks of untainted snow, whose summits reached to heights of twenty-five thousand, twenty-six thousand, and, in one supreme case, twenty-eight thousand feet above sea-level. There was this wonderful array of mountain majesty set out before me across a deep rock-bound valley, and away in the distance, filling up the

head, could be seen a vast glacier, the out-
pourings of the mountain masses which give it
birth.   It was a scene which, as I viewed it,
and realised that this seemingly impregnable
array must be pierced and overcome, seemed to
put the iron into my soul and stiffen up all my
energies for the task which lay before me.

Buried in the stirring feelings to which such
a scene gives rise, I sat there for more than an
hour, till the caravan arrived, and then we
slowly descended from the pass into the valley
bottom at our feet.   The way was rough and
steep, but we reached the banks of the river
without any serious difficulty.   Here, however,
we were brought to a standstill, for there was a
sheer cliff of a couple of hundred feet or so in
height running far away on either hand along
the river's edge.   This at first seemed a serious
obstacle, but I had noticed on the way down
some tracks of kyang (wild asses), and as there
was no water above, I knew that these animals
must get down to the river to drink some way
or other, and that where they could go we
could go also.   I therefore went back to these
tracks, carefully followed them up, and was
relieved to find they led down a practicable

"shoot" in the cliff. It was very steep and rocky, but by unloading the ponies, and putting one man on to lead each in front and two others to hold on to the tail behind, we managed to let the ponies down one by one, and after a good deal of labour found ourselves, bag and baggage, on the edge of a river, which in some ways might be considered the main branch of the Yarkand River.

This tributary, which the Baltis with me called the Shaksgam, but which the Kirghiz seem to know as the Oprang, was previously unknown. It rises among the glaciers of the main watershed. Two years later I followed it down to its junction with the other branch of the Yarkand River.

We continued down the valley of the Oprang (Shaksgam) River, till we came to another stream, which my Baltis called the Sarpo Laggo, flowing down from the main range and joining it on the left bank. This we ascended till we reached a patch of jungle called Suget Jangal. Just before arriving there I chanced to look up rather suddenly, and a sight met my eyes which fairly staggered me. We had just turned a corner which brought into view, on the left hand, a peak of appalling height, which could be none other than K.2, 28,278 feet in height, second only to Mount Everest as the highest mountain in the world.   Viewed from this direction, it appeared to rise in an almost perfect cone, but to an inconceivable height. We were quite close under it—perhaps not a dozen miles from its summit—and here on the northern side, where it is literally clothed in glacier, it must have been covered for from fourteen to sixteen thousand feet with solid ice. It was one of those sights which impress a man for ever, and produce a lasting sense of the greatness and grandeur of Nature's works— which he can never lose or forget.

For some time I stood apart, absorbed in the contemplation of this wonderful sight, and then we marched on past Suget Jangal till we reached the foot of the great glacier which flows down from the Mustagh Pass.   Here we bivouacked.   The tussle with these mountain giants was now to reach its climax, and our subsequent adventures I must leave to a separate chapter.

CHAPTER IX.

THE MUSTAGH PASS.

" The palaces of nature, whose vast walls
　　Have pinnacled in clouds their snowy scalps
　　And throned eternity in. icy halls
　　Of cold sublimity, where forms and falls
　　The avalanche—the thunderbolt of snow !
　　All that expands the spirit, yet appals,
　　Gather around those summits, as to show
How earth may reach to heaven, yet leave vain man below."
　　　　　　　　　　　　　　　—*Byron.*

THE Mustagh Pass, which we were now approaching, is on the main watershed, which
both divides the rivers of India from the rivers
of Turkestan, and also the British from the
Chinese dominions. Peaks along the watershed, in the vicinity of the pass, had been
fixed by trigonometrical observations from
the Indian side at 24,000, 26,000, and as we
have seen in one case at over 28,000 feet in
height, so I could scarcely doubt that the pass
across the range must be lofty and difficult. It

was, therefore, all the more worth conquering, and as it would be the final and greatest obstacle on my long journey from Peking, I set out to tackle it with the determination to overcome it at almost any cost. Every other difficulty had been successfully negotiated, and this last remaining obstacle, though the most severe of all, was not to be permitted at the climax of my journey to keep me from my goal.

These were my feelings as I advanced up the valley, at the head of which lay the Mustagh Pass. But I had little idea of the magnitude of the difficulties which in reality lay before me, and these were soon to commence.

Scarcely a mile from our bivouac of the previous night we came to a point where the valley was blocked by what appeared to be enormous heaps of broken stones and fragments of rock. These heaps were between two and three hundred feet in height, and stretched completely across the valley. I had gone on ahead by myself, and when I saw these mounds of *débris*, I thought we might have trouble in taking ponies over such rough obstacles; but I was altogether taken aback when, on coming up to the heaps, I found that they were masses of solid ice, merely covered over on the surface with a thin layer of this rocky *débris*, which served to conceal the surface of the ice immediately beneath. And my dismay can be imagined when, on ascending one of the highest of the mounds, I found that they were but the end of a series which extended without interruption for many miles up the valley to the snows at the foot of the pass. We were, in fact, at the extremity of an immense glacier. This was the first time I had actually stood on a glacier, and I had never realised till now how huge and continuous a mass of ice it is. Here and there, breaking through the mounds of stone, I had seen cliffs of what I thought was black rock, but on coming close up to these found them to be nothing but solid dark green ice. I discovered caverns, too, with transparent walls of clear, clean ice, and long, tapering icicles hanging in delicate fringes from the roof. It was an astonishing and wonderful sight ; but I was destined to see yet more marvellous scenes than this in the icy region upon which I was now entering.

To take a caravan of ponies up a glacier like

this seemed to me an utter impossibility. The guides thought so too, and I decided upon sending the ponies round by the Karakoram Pass, 180 miles to the eastward, to Leh, and going on myself over the Mustagh Pass with a couple of men. This would have been a risky proceeding, for if we did not find our way over the pass we should have scarcely enough provisions with us to last us till we could return to an inhabited place again. Supplies altogether were running short, and the longer we took in reaching the pass, the harder we should fare if we did not succeed in getting over. But while I was deciding upon sending the ponies back, the caravan men were making a gallant attempt to lead them up the glacier. I rejoined them, and we all helped the ponies along as well as we could; hauling at them in front, pushing at them behind, and sometimes unloading and ourselves carrying the loads up the stone-covered mounds of ice. But it was terribly hard and trying work for the animals. They could get no proper foothold, and as they kept climbing up the sides of a mound they would scratch away the thin layer of stones on the surface, and then, coming on to the pure ice immediately below, would slip and fall and cut their knees and hocks about in a way which went directly to my heart. I did not see how this sort of thing could last. We had only advanced a few hundred yards, and there were still from fifteen to twenty miles of glacier ahead. I therefore halted the ponies for the day, and went on with a couple of men to reconnoitre. We fortunately found, in between the glacier and the mountain-side, a narrow stretch of less impracticable ground, along which it would be possible to take the ponies. This we marked out, and returned to our bivouac after dark.

That night we passed, as usual, in the open, thoroughly exhausted after the hard day's work, for at the high altitudes we had now reached the rarefaction of the air makes one tired very quickly, and the constant tumbling about on the slippery glacier in helping the ponies over it added to one's troubles. My boots were cut through, my hands cut all over, and my elbows a mass of bruises.

At daybreak on the following morning we started again, leading the ponies up the route we had marked out ; but a mile from the point where our previous exploration had ended we

were confronted by another great glacier flowing
down from the left. We now had a glacier on
one side of us, mountains on the other, and a
second glacier right across our front. At this
time my last remaining pair of boots were completely worn out, and my feet so sore from the
bruises they received on the glacier I could
scarcely bear to put them to the ground. So
I stayed behind with the ponies, while two men
went on to find a way through the obstacles
before us. The men returned after a time, and
said they could find no possible way for the
ponies ; but they begged me to have a look
myself, saying that perhaps by my good fortune
I might be able to find one.

I accordingly, with a couple of men, retraced
my steps down the edge of the main glacier
for some little distance, till we came to a point
where it was possible to get ponies on to the
glacier itself and take them right out into the
middle. We then ascended a prominent spot
on the glacier, from which we could obtain a
good view all round. We were in a sea of
ice. There was now little of the rocky moraine
stuff with which the ice of the glacier had been
covered in its lower part, and we looked out on

a vast river of pure white ice, broken up into myriads of sharp needle-like points. Snowy mountains rose above us on either hand, and down their sides rolled the lesser glaciers, like clotted cream pouring over the lip of a cream-jug; and rising forbiddingly before us was the cold icy range we should have to cross.

This, marvellous as it was to look upon, was scarcely the country through which to take a caravan of ponies, but I made out a line of moraine extending right up the main glacier. We got on to this, and, following it up for some distance, found, to our great relief, that it would be quite possible to bring ponies up it on to the smooth snow of the *névé* at the head of the glacier. Having ascertained this beyond a doubt, we returned late in the afternoon towards the spot where we had left our ponies. Darkness, however, overtook us before we reached it. We wandered about on the glacier for some time, and nearly lost our way; but at last, quite worn out, reached our little caravan once more.

That night we held a council of war as to which of the two Mustagh Passes we should attack. There are two passes, known as the

Mustagh, which cross the range. One, to the east, that is to our left as we were ascending the glacier, is known as the Old Mustagh Pass, and was in use in former days, till the advance of ice upon it made it so difficult that a new one was sought for, and what is known as the New Mustagh Pass, some ten miles farther west along the range, had been discovered. It was over this latter pass that the guides hoped to conduct our party. They said that even ponies had in former times been taken across it by means of ropes and by making rough bridges across the crevasses. No European had crossed either of them, but Colonel Godwin-Austen, in 1862, reached the southern foot of the new pass in the course of his survey of Baltistan. This New Mustagh Pass seemed the more promising of the two, and I therefore decided upon sending two men on the following morning to reconnoitre it and report upon its practicability.

At the first streak of daylight the reconnoiterers set out, and the remainder of us afterwards followed with the ponies along the route which we had explored on the previous day. We took the ponies up the glacier without any

serious difficulty, and in the evening halted
close up to the head of the glacier where
snowy mountains of stupendous height shut
us in on every hand.   At dusk the two men
who had been sent out to reconnoitre the
new pass returned, to say that the ice had so
accumulated on it that it would be now quite
impossible to take ponies over, and that it
would be difficult even for men to cross it.
The plan which they therefore suggested was
to leave the ponies behind, and cross the range
by the Old Mustagh Pass, push on to Askoli,
the first village on the south side of the range,
and from there send back men with supplies
for the ponies and the men with them sufficient
to enable the caravan to reach Shahidula, on
the usual trade route beteen Yarkand and
Kashmir.   This was evidently all we could do.
We could not take the ponies any farther, and
we could not send them back as they were,
for we had nearly run out of supplies, and
Shahidula the nearest point at which fresh
supplies could be obtained, was one hundred
and eighty miles distant.   All now depended
upon our being able to cross the pass.   If we
were not able to, we should have to march this

one hundred and eighty miles back through the
mountains with only three or four days' supplies
to support us.   We might certainly have eaten
the ponies, so would not actually have starved ;
but we should have had a hard struggle for it,
and there would still have been the range to
cross at another point.

Matters were therefore approaching a critical
stage, and that was an anxious night for me.
I often recall it, and think of our little bivouac
in the snow at the foot of the range we had to
overcome.   The sun sank behind the icy
mountains, the bright glow gently disappeared,
and they became steely hard while the grey
cold of night settled shimmering down upon
them.   All around was pure white snow and
ice, breathing out cold upon us.   The little
pools and streamlets of water which the heat of
the sun had poured off the glacier during the
day were now gripped by the frost, which
seemed to creep around ourselves too, and
huddle us up together.   We had no tent to
shelter us from the biting streams of air flowing
down from the mountain summits, and we had
not sufficient fuel to light a fire round which we
might lie.   We had, indeed, barely enough

Q

brushwood to keep up a fire for cooking; but my Chinese servant cooked a simple meal of rice and mutton for us all. We gathered round the fire to eat it hot out of the bowl, and then rolled ourselves up in our sheepskins and went to sleep, with the stars twinkling brightly above, and the frost gripping closer and closer upon us.

Next morning, while it was yet dark, Wali, the guide, awoke us. We each had a drink of tea and some bread, and then we started off to attack the pass. The ponies, with nearly all the baggage, were left behind under the charge of Liu-san, the Chinaman, and some of the older men. All we took with us was a roll of bedding for myself, a sheepskin coat for each man, some native biscuits, tea and a large tea-kettle, and a bottle of brandy. The ascent to the pass was easy but trying, for we were now not far from nineteen thousand feet above sea-level, and at that height, walking uphill through deep snow, we quickly became exhausted. We could only take a dozen or twenty steps at a time, and we would then bend over on our sticks and pant as if we had been running hard uphill. We were tantalised, too, by the

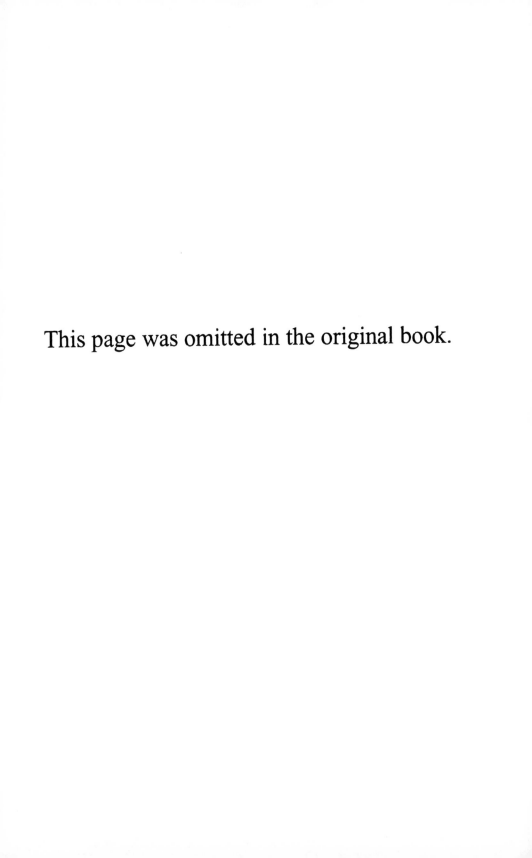
This page was omitted in the original book.

CAMP ON A GLACIER—MUSTAGH PASS.   *Page* 226.

What, however, saved our party was my
holding my tongue. I kept quite silent as I
looked over the pass, and waited to hear what
the men had to say about it. They meanwhile
were looking at me, and, imagining that an
Englishman never went back from an enterprise he had once started on, took it as a
matter of course that, as I gave no order to go
back, I necessarily meant to go on. So they
set about their preparations for the descent.
We had brought an ordinary pickaxe with us,
and Wali went on ahead with this, while the
rest of us followed one by one behind him, each
hanging on to a rope tied round Wali's waist to
support him in case he slipped while hewing
steps across an ice-slope leading to a rocky
precipice which seemed to afford the only
possible means of descending the pass. This
slope was of hard ice, very steep, and, thirty
yards or so below the line we took, ended in an
ice-fall, which again terminated many hundreds
of feet beneath in the head of a glacier at the
foot of the pass. Wali with his pickaxe hewed
a way step by step across the ice-slope, so as to
reach the rocky cliff by which we should have
to descend on to the glacier below.

CROSSING AN ICE-SLOPE ON THE MUSTAGH PASS.

Page 228.

We slowly edged across the slope after him,
but it was hard to keep cool and steady.   From
where we stood we could see nothing over the
end of the slope but the glacier hundreds of
feet below us.   Some of the men were so little
nervous that they kicked the fragments of ice
hewed out by Wali down the slope, and laughed
as they saw them hop down it and with one
last bound disappear altogether.   But an almost
sickening feeling came on me as I watched
this, for we were standing on a slope as steep
as the roof of a house.   We had no ice-axes
with which to anchor ourselves or give us
support ; and though I tied handkerchiefs, and
the men bits of leather and cloth, round the
insteps of our smooth native boots, to give us
a little grip on the slippery ice, I could not
help feeling that if any one of us had lost his
foothold the rest would never have been able
to hold him up with the rope, and that in all
likelihood the whole party would have been
carried away and plunged into the abyss below.

Outwardly I kept as cool and cheerful as I
could, but inwardly I shuddered at each fresh
step I took.   The sun was now pouring down
and just melted the surface of the steps after

they were hewn, so that by the time those of us who were a few paces behind Wali reached a step the ice was just covered over with water and this made it still more slippery for our soft leather boots, which had now become almost slimy on the surface. It was under these circumstances that my Ladaki servant Drogpa gave in. He was shaking all over in an exaggerated shiver, and so unsteady, I thought he would slip at any moment and perhaps carry us all with him. We were but at the beginning of our trials. We had not even begun the actual descent yet, but were merely crossing to a point from which we should make it. And to have such a man with us might have endangered the safety of the whole party; so I told him he might return to the ponies and go round with them. It rather upset me to see a born hillman so affected, but I pretended not to care a bit and laughed it off, *pour encourager les autres*, as the thing had to be done.

At last we reached the far side of the slope, and found ourselves on a projecting piece of rock protruding through the ice. Here we could rest, but only with the prospect of still

further difficulties before us. We were at the
head of the rocky precipice, the face of which
we should have to descend to reach the ice-
slopes which extended to the glacier at the foot
of the pass. At such heights as those which
we had now reached, where the snow and ice
lie sometimes hundreds of feet thick, it is only
where it is very steep that the bare rock shows
through. The cliff we had now to descend
was an almost sheer precipice; its only saving
feature was that it was rough and rugged, and
so afforded some little hold for our hands and
feet. Yet even then we seldom got a hold for
the whole hand or whole foot. All we generally found was a little ledge, upon which we
could grip with the tips of the fingers or side
of the foot. The men were most good to
me, whenever possible guiding my foot into
some secure hold, and often supporting it there
with their hands; but at times it was all I
could do to summon sufficient courage to let
myself down on to the veriest little crevices
which had to support me. There was a constant dread, too, that fragments of these ledges
might give way with the weight upon them;
for the rock was very crumbly, as it generally

is when exposed to severe frosts, and once I
heard a shout from above, as a huge piece of
rock which had been detached came crashing
past me, and as nearly as possible hit two of
the men who had already got half-way down.

We reached the bottom of the cliff without
accident, and then found ourselves at the head
of a long ice-slope extending down to the
glacier below. Protruding through the ice
were three pieces of rock, which would serve
us as successive halting-places, and we determined upon taking a line which led by them.
We had brought with us every scrap of rope
that could be spared from the ponies' gear, and
we tied these and all the men's turbans and
waist-clothes together into one long rope, by
which we let a man down the ice-slope on to
the first projecting rock. As he went down he
cut steps, and when he had reached the rock
we tied the upper end of the rope firmly on to
a rock above, and then one by one we came
down the slope, hanging on to the rope and
making use of the steps which had been cut.
This was, therefore, a comparatively easy part
of the descent; but one man was as nearly as
possible lost. He slipped, fell over on his back,

and came sliding down the slope at a frightful pace. Luckily, however, he still managed to keep hold of the rope with one hand, and so kept himself from dashing over the ice-fall at the side of the slope ; but when he reached the rock his hand was almost bared of skin, and he was shivering with fright. Wali, however, gave him a sound rating for being so careless, and on the next stage made him do all the hardest part of the work.

The other men got down the slope without mishap, and then came the last man. He, of course, could not have the benefit of a rope to hang on by, for he would have to untie it from the rock and bring it with him. Wali had selected for this, the most dangerous piece of work in the whole descent, the man who had especially troubled me by knocking pieces of ice over the precipice when we were on the ice-slope at the head of the pass. He was one of the slaves I had released at Yarkand; an incessant grumbler, and very rough, but, next to Wali, the best man I had for any really hard work. He tied the end of the rope round his waist, and then slowly and carefully came down the steps which had been hewn in the slope.

We at the end of the rope pulled it in at every step he took, so that if he slipped, though he might fall past us, we should be able to haul in the rope fast, and so perhaps save him from the ice-fall. He reached our rock of refuge in safety, and we then in the same manner descended two more stages of the ice-slope, and finally reached a part where the slope was less steep, and we could proceed without cutting steps the whole way.

At last, just as the sun set, we reached the glacier at the foot of the pass. We were in safety once more. The tension of six crucial hours was over, and the last and greatest obstacle in my journey had been successfully surmounted. Those moments when I stood at the foot of the pass are long to be remembered by me—moments of intense relief, of glowing pride and of deep gratitude for the success that had been granted. But such feelings as mine were now cannot be described in words; they are known only to those who have had their heart set on one great object and have accomplished it.

I took a last look at the pass, never before nor since seen by a European, and which, viewed

from below, looked utterly impracticable to any
human being.   Then we started away down
the glacier to find some bare spot on which to
lay our rugs and rest.

The sun had now set, but, fortunately for us,
there was an abundance of light, and the night
was marvellously beautiful, so that, tired as I
was, I could not but be impressed by it.   The
moon was nearly full, the sky without a cloud,
and in the amphitheatre of snowy mountains
and among the icy seracs of the glacier, not one
speck of anything but the purest white was
visible.   The air at these altitudes, away from
dust and with no misty vapour in it, was absolutely clear, and the soft silvery rays of the
moon struck down upon the glistening mountains in unsullied radiance.   The whole effect
was of some enchanting fairy scene ; and the
sternness of the mountains was slowly softened
down till lost, and their beauty in its purest
form alone remained.

With our senses enervated by such a scene as
this, and overcome with delight as we were at
having successfully crossed the pass, we pushed
on down the glacier in a dreamy, careless way,
perfectly regardless of the dangers which lay

hidden around us.   Under ordinary circumstances we should have proceeded cautiously
down a glacier which, beautiful though it was,
had its full share of crevasses ; and it was only
when I turned round and found one man missing, that I realised how negligent we had been.
We retraced our steps, and found the poor
fellow had dropped down a crevasse, the mouth
of which had been covered with a thin coating
of ice and snow, which had given way under
his weight, so that he had dropped through.
Very fortunately the crevasse was not wide,
and after falling about fifteen feet he had been
wedged in between the two sides by the load of
my bedding which he was carrying; so by
letting a rope down we were able to extricate
him in safety.   This taught us a lesson, and
for the rest of the way we went along roped
together, as we ought to have been from the
first, and tested each step as we advanced.

I now kept in the rear, and the man with my
bedding was in front of me.   As we were closed
up during a temporary halt, I detected a strong
smell of brandy coming from the bundle of
bedding.   A distracting thought occurred to me.
I tore open the bundle, and there was my last

bottle of brandy—broken! Lady Walsham, on my leaving Peking, had insisted upon giving me at least two bottles of brandy for the journey. I had drunk one in the Gobi Desert, and I had made up my mind to keep the other till the day I had crossed the Mustagh Pass, but there it was broken, and the brandy wasted, just when both the men and myself were really needing something to pull us together. The bundle of bedding had been thrown over the pass to save carrying it down, and though the bottle had been wrapped up in my sheepskin sleeping-bag, it had been smashed to pieces.

About eleven o'clock we at last reached a piece of ground on the mountain-side free from snow, and here we halted for the night. There was no wood, and only a few roots of weeds about with which to light a fire, so we had to break up a couple of our alpenstocks to make a small fire, by which we managed to boil sufficient water to make a few cups of tea. We had some buscuit with that, and then I got into my sheepskin bag, and the men wrapped themselves up in their sheepskin coats, and we lay down and slept as if nothing could ever wake us again. The work and anxiety on the

last few days had been great, and on this day
we had been on the move for eighteen hours
continuously.   Now the worst was over, and I
slept with my mind at ease and happy.

But at daybreak the next morning we were
on our legs again.   We had still a long way to
go before we could reach Askoli, the nearest
village, and our men remaining behind on the
pass were waiting for supplies.   Yet freezing as
it was we had to start without anything to warm
us, for we could find no materials for a fire ;
but at about ten o'clock, at a point near where
our glacier joined the great Baltoro glacier, we
found an old hut, built at the time when this
route was in use, and from the fragments of
wood about we made up the first good fire we
had had for a week past, and had a fairly
substantial meal.   But we could not indulge
ourselves at all freely, for we were very short
of provisions.   We had left with the men on
the pass all but just sufficient to carry us
through to Askoli ; and a few mouthfuls of
meat, with some biscuit and some tea, were all
we could allow ourselves.   Having eaten this
and rested for an hour, we again pushed on,
and struck the Baltoro glacier nearly opposite

the great Masher Brum peak, which stands up over twenty-five thousand feet high just across the glacier.   Then, turning to our left in the opposite direction to Askoli, we could see far away up this, the largest mountain glacier in the world, other peaks of even greater height, rising like snowy spires in the distance.   Four peaks over twenty-six thousand feet, stand out at the head of the Baltoro glacier, and away to our left, though hidden from us, was the peak K.2, which I had seen from the northern side of the Mustagh Pass.   Five years afterwards, Sir William Conway's party explored the entire length of the glacier, and ascended a peak twenty-three thousand feet in height at its head; but, fascinating though it would have been to have wandered among these mountain giants, in a region unsurpassed for sublimity and grandeur by any in the world, I could only now think of reaching an inhabited spot again as rapidly as possible.

We turned to the right, then down the glacier, keeping along the moraine close to the mountain-side.   This and the two following were days of agony to me, for my native boots were now in places worn through till the bare

skin of my foot was exposed, and I had to
hobble along on my toes or my heels to keep
the worn-out part by the balls of my feet from
the sharp stones and rocky *débris* of the glacier.
On account of this tenderness of my feet, I was
always slipping, too, falling and bruising my
elbows, or cutting my hands on the rough
stones in trying to save myself.

All that day we plodded wearily along down
the glacier, till at sunset we came upon a little
clump of fir trees on the mountain-side.   Here
we were able to make up as big a fire as we
wished, and if we could only have had more
to eat, would have been perfectly happy ; but
there was now no meat left, and tea and biscuit
was all we had.   Next day we reached the end
of the glacier, and sleeping that night in a cave,
on the following day made our last march into
Askoli.   Never did I think we were going to
reach that spot !   By midday we saw its green
trees and fields in the distance ; but I could
only drag myself slowly along, as the way was
rough and stony, and I was footsore and exhausted.   At last, however, at four o'clock, we
really entered the village.   We sent for the
headman, and told him to bring us some food.

A bed was brought me to lie on, and then, with a stewed fowl and some rice to eat, fresh life and energy came into me, and I could realise the satisfaction of having reached the first inhabited spot in Indian territory.

But that was a dirty little village! The trees and the fields looked fresh and green, and were a delight to us after the cold and barren mountains, but the houses and the inhabitants were repulsively dirty; and the latter by no means well-disposed. Mountain people are always nervous about strangers, and these had thought the way into their country from the north was entirely closed, and did not at all welcome this living proof that it was not. Wali, the guide, was himself a native of the village, which he had left some thirty years before. Another of my men also belonged to it. But they said they feared the people would do them some injury for having shown me the way, and they kept by me constantly, and left the village with me, subsequently returning to Yarkand by Leh and the Karakoram Pass, instead of directly by the Mustagh Pass, as they might have done.

Immediately we had had something to eat,

R

we set about preparing to send back supplies to the men and ponies on the other side of Mustagh Pass. With great difficulty we induced the people to do this; and on the following day a party was started off back towards the Mustagh Pass. They took with them ropes and poles, and though three men were badly injured in doing so, they succeeded in crossing the pass and giving my men the needful supplies.

I would now willingly have had a rest, but, though I could not start on the day following our arrival, for I was seriously unwell from having, in the excess of my hunger, eaten too much of the messy greasy dishes the inhabitants had provided for me, on the day after I set out to explore the other Mustagh Pass—what is called the New Mustagh Pass. It was depressing, just as I had reached the first village on the Indian side, to have to turn my back on India; but I did not like to leave this pass untried, and with Wali and a party of men from Askoli we set out on the second day after our arrival to explore it.

These men of Askoli were in dread of the mountains, and on the first evening, at the foot of a mountain whose summit was supposed to be the abode of a guardian deity, they, although Mohammedans, sacrificed a bullock to this deity, and prayed and salaamed to it. As they subsequently ate the bullock, and as I paid for it, this little ceremony was doubtless very helpful to them. At any rate, they were much more cheerful after it, and as I now had some new foot-gear, we were able to push along rapidly up the Punmah glacier. But on the third day from Askoli, opposite a camping-ground called Skinmang, we were brought to a standstill. At this point the glacier flowing down from the New Mustagh Pass joins the Punmah glacier, and we were completely "cornered" between the two glaciers. To reach the pass we should have had to cross the glacier flowing down from it; but this we found it impossible to do, for just at this point there had evidently been an immense ice-slip on to the glacier, and gigantic blocks of ice were tumbled about one on the top of the other in a way which made it perfectly impossible to get any footing at all on the glacier. So we turned round and faced for Askoli once more.

I think now of that wonderful glacier region,

and the amphitheatre of snowy peaks at the head of the Punmah glacier, and recall all the marvellous beauties of a scene such as can only be witnessed in a few rarely visited spots on the face of the earth, but at the time my thoughts were almost entirely directed towards India. I was wearied out with my struggle with the mountains, and longed to be free of them and at rest once more.

On the day after our return to Askoli, the men who had been sent by the Old Mustagh Pass to the party with the ponies arrived back also. They had handed over the supplies to them, and Liu-san, Drogpa, and the rest had started off to take the ponies round by the Karakoram Pass to Leh. Having satisfied myself about this, I set out by double marches for Kashmir and the Punjab.

We followed down the valley of the Braldo River till it joined the open Shigar valley, and here at last I was able to mount a pony again, and, instead of plodding wearily along, to travel in comfort and enjoy the wonderful scenery around me. How great a difference one's mere animal feelings make in the ability to appreciate the beauties of nature! Worn and tired out, it was only something unusually striking that had produced any impression upon me, and I would pass by peaks of marvellous grandeur with only a weary upward glance at them, and sometimes even a longing that they had never existed to bar my way and keep me from my journey's end. But now, seated on the back of a pony—miserable little animal though it was—I had no longer that load of weariness weighing upon me, and could quietly drink in all the pleasure which looking on that glorious mountain scenery gives.

The Shigar valley is from two to three miles broad; its bottom is covered over with village lands, where apricot trees are grown in hundreds, and these trees now, in the autumn season, were clothed in foliage of every lovely tint of red and purple and yellow. This mass of bright warm foliage filled the valley bottom, then above it rose the bare rugged mountainsides, and crowning these the everlasting snows. The sun shone out in an unclouded, deep-blue sky; the icy blasts of the Mustagh were left behind for good and all; and we were in an ideal climate, with no extremes of either heat

or cold to try us. The grave, anxious look
on the men's faces passed away; they now
stepped cheerily along by my side chaffing
over all the difficulties they had gone through,
and, at each village we came to, taking a fill
of dried apricots and grapes and walnuts, so
plentiful in this fruitful valley.

The country we were now in was Baltistan,
the inhabitants of which—called Baltis—are a
patient, docile, good-natured race, whom one
hardly respects, but whom one cannot help
liking in a compassionate, pitying way. The
poor Balti belongs to one of those races which
has gone under in the struggle of nations. In
their better days the Baltis are said to have
been able to fight well; but their fighting days
are past. They could not resist the Dogra
invasion from Kashmir; and now they are
ruled by a foreign race, and because they were
such good carriers, and because the roads
through their own and the adjoining countries
were so bad, it fell out that they were employed
more and more for carrying purposes, till the
patient, long-suffering Balti coolie became a
well-known feature in the valleys of this
frontier.

There is little that is strong or masculine
about the Balti to cause one to admire him,
but yet one likes him for his very patience
and the ease with which he can be pleased.
And among these Baltis I have employed,
have been some for whom I have borne respect
for their intense devotion to what they believed
to be their duty. I now was on the eve of
parting with those five who brought me over
the Mustagh Pass, and for Wali, their headman, I entertain a regard such as I do for few
other men.

I picture him now as he was first brought
before me at the inn at Yarkand—a short,
thick-set man, with an iron-grey beard, a
prominent, rather hooked nose, and an expression of determination and proud indifference to danger about his chin and underlip.
Asked if he were willing to conduct me over
the Mustagh Pass, he replied that he did not
want to go, but if he were really required
he would undertake to guide me ; the only
condition he would make would be that I
should not look at a map! He had heard
Englishmen were inclined to guide themselves
and trust the map rather than the man with

them ; if I was going to do that, I might, but he would not go with me. On the other hand, if I would trust him, he would take me safely over. On this understanding I engaged him. No one could have more loyally carried out his compact, and but for him we should never have been able to cross the Mustagh Pass. He went to work in a steady, self-reliant way which gave everyone confidence, and all the men looked up to him and obeyed him implicitly.

The more I see of men like him, the more convinced I am, that weak in many respects though such men as these Baltis are, yet if once they are given responsibility, shown trust, and left to work out their own salvation, they develop many latent qualities which probably neither they nor anybody else believed to be in them. Old Wali went back to Yarkand by Leh, and three years later, when I again visited Yarkand, he came to see me, looking precisely the same, and dressed, I believe, in the very same clothes as when we had parted, and it was a real pleasure to see again a man who had done me such loyal service.

Another of the Baltis who had done excellent work was the slave whose release I had purchased at Yarkand. He was a wild-looking character, but the hardest-working man I have ever known. Now that he had regained his freedom, was being liberally paid, and was on his way home, he did not mind how much work he did, and all through the march from Yarkand he behaved splendidly. We passed by his native village one day as we were marching through Baltistan, and left him there. But on the following day he caught us up again, carrying an immense load of fruit and provision for a big dinner for the men. He had brought all this twelve miles, and he came and kissed my hands and feet, and said he could not allow us to go away without showing how grateful he felt. These Baltis are a warm-hearted people when once their deeper feelings can be reached, and when their hearts have not been crushed out of them by that fatal load-carrying, and I parted from my faithful followers with sincere regret.

A few marches farther on I crossed my last pass, the Zoji-la, eleven thousand four hundred feet high. It was perfectly easy, and then on descending the southern side the aspect of the mountains suddenly changed. Hitherto, from far away at their rise from the Yarkand plains, the mountains had been barren and destitute of any trace of forest. Occasionally in some favoured sheltered spot a dwarfed tree or two might be seen, but as a whole it was only in the valley bottoms and on cultivated lands that any trees were met with. Now the transformation was complete. We had reached the southern-facing slopes of the outward ridge of the Himalayas, and upon these slopes all the rains of the monsoon are expended. Consequently while on the northern side are bare sun-baked rocks only, on the southern side the mountain slopes are densely packed with forest.

We passed rapidly down the beautifully wooded Sind valley, with its meadows and pine forests, its rushing torrents and snow-clad mountain summits, and at last reached the open valley of Kashmir itself. Some seven or eight miles' march brought us to Srinagar, that most picturesquely situated but dirtiest of all towns, and then for the first time I realised how very dirty I myself was, and how rough I had become. Dressed in a Yarkand

THE SIND VALLEY, KASHMIR.   *Page* 250.

sheepskin coat and long Yarkand boots, with
a round Tam-o'-shanter cap as the only European article of dress about me, with a rough
beard, and my face burnt by exposure in the
desert and cut and reddened by the cold on
the glaciers, I was addressed by the people of
the place as a Yarkandi. My first care, therefore, was to go off to one of the native shops
which provide all necessaries for Europeans,
and purchase a clean shirt and a knickerbocker
suit, such as officers wear out shooting in
Kashmir, and to have my hair cut, my beard
shaved off, and get a good wash. When I had
expended nearly two hours upon these preparations for my plunge into civilisation, I went
to see Captain Ramsay, the political agent on
duty at Srinagar at the time. It was very trying,
therefore, when Captain Ramsay, almost immediately after shaking hands, said, " Wouldn't
you like to have a wash?" This was the first
of the many shocks I had on returning to
civilisation.

But there were some pleasant surprises too,
and I remember the satisfaction I felt at receiv-
ing a telegram at Srinagar, conveying to me
the congratulations of Lord Roberts, the then

commander-in-chief, upon my having successfully accomplished the journey, and a very kind
letter from General Chapman, then Quartermaster-General in India, who had himself been
to Yarkand and Kashgar, and, knowing how
welcome they are to travellers, had thoughtfully
sent a box of cigars to await my arrival.

Only one day was given up for rest in
Srinagar, and then I started on the last stage
of my journey, that to Rawal Pindi; for I was
anxious to accomplish my task in precisely the
seven months which I had said at Peking
would be the time necessary for it, and which
would expire on November the 4th. So I
hurried on, and now at the end of a long
journey felt "fitter" than when I started, and
able to cover the distance rapidly. After
arriving at a staging bungalow at seven o'clock
on the evening of November 2, I had my
dinner, lay down for an hour or two, and then
at twelve o'clock at night started again walking
the first march of twelve miles, and afterwards
riding in a native cart, which conveyed me
during the day for three marches down the
newly constructed cart-road. At the end of
these three marches I rode another ten miles

uphill towards Murree, and arrived at a dak
bungalow at sunset.   Here I rested for part of
the night, but at three o'clock in the morning
started again, marching the ten miles into Murree on foot.   From there in a tonga I drove
rapidly down the last thirty-nine miles into
Rawal Pindi.   The change was wonderful.   I
had thought riding a miserable native pony a
luxury in comparison with the weary marching
on foot.   Then trundling along at a jog-trot in
a native cart on the Kashmir road had seemed
the very essence of all that was comfortable.
But now I was in a conveyance with a pair of
ponies galloping down the hill, and with what
seemed perfect rest to me was covering every
hour three or four times the distance I had
been able to accomplish on foot.   Still better, I
was freeing myself from the nightmare of the
mountains, and, in place of the never-ending
barriers of ranges blocking the way and shutting
me in, there was stretched out before me the
wide open plains of the Punjab.   From the
plains of Turkestan on the one side, I had made
my way through the labyrinth of mountains,
over one range after another, past each suc-
ceeding obstacle, till I had now reached the

plains on the southern side. My whole long
journey from Peking was at an end.   My
utmost hopes had been fulfilled, and in precisely
the time I had laid out for the enterprise I had
reached that destination which, as I rode forth
from the gates of Peking, had seemed so remote
and inaccessible.   On April 4 I left Peking, and
on November 4 I drove up to the mess-house
of my regiment at Rawal Pindi, and received
the congratulations of Colonel Thompson and
my brother officers.

Poor Liu-san, the Chinese servant, arrived
six weeks later with the ponies, which we had
been obliged to send back from the Mustagh
Pass round by the Karakoram and Leh.   He
was suffering badly from pleurisy, brought on
by exposure ; but when he was sufficiently
recovered he was sent back to China by sea,
and he afterwards accompanied the persevering
American traveller, Mr. Rockhill, to Tibet.
He was a Chinaman, and therefore not a
perfect animal, but he understood his business
thoroughly, and he did it.   So for a journey
across the entire breadth of the Chinese Empire I could scarcely have found a better man.
As long as he felt that he was "running" me,

and that it was his business to convey me, like a bundle of goods, from one side of China to the other, he worked untiringly. And the success of the journey is in no small degree due to this single servant, who had served me loyally, and had not feared to accompany me throughout.

From Rawal Pindi I proceeded to Simla, and there saw Colonel Bell, from whom I had parted at Peking, and who, travelling more rapidly than I did, had reached India a month before. To him, therefore, belongs the honour of being the first European to reach India from China by land. But I think I may fairly claim for myself the distinction of being the only human being who has travelled continuously through, from the shores of the Pacific on the one side to the plains of India on the other. From the Manchurian port of Possiet Bay, and from the banks of the Sungari, I had made my way across the entire breadth of the Chinese Empire, and had now reached the first cantonment in British India.

I had travelled for nigh upon seven thousand miles over the richly-cultivated lands of Manchuria and the barren Desert of Gobi, through

the gloomy forests of the Ever-White Mountain
and the bounding prairies of Mongolia, over
the level plains of Turkestan, and across the
loftiest range of mountains in the world. I had
experienced every kind of climate—drenching
rains and a dryness inconceivable to a dweller
in Europe ; the scorching heat of a desert
summer, and the biting cold of a Himalayan
glacier. I had found shelter in Chinese inns,
in Manchurian farmhouses, in the rude huts of
the forest sable-hunters, in a Cossack colonel's
quarters, the palatial residence of our minister
at Peking, the felt tents of the nomad tribes,
and the mud-houses of Central Asian villagers ;
and lastly, in the severest part of all for weeks,
in crossing the Himalayas, I had slept entirely
in the open without even a tent.

If the knowledge thus hardly acquired can be
of value to others ; if, in the future, experiences
gained while I was but twenty-four can help me
as they have in the past, I shall feel doubly
repaid for whatever hardships I may have
endured. And I can even now feel that those
few full months of toil and stress have brought
to me a life-enduring pleasure.

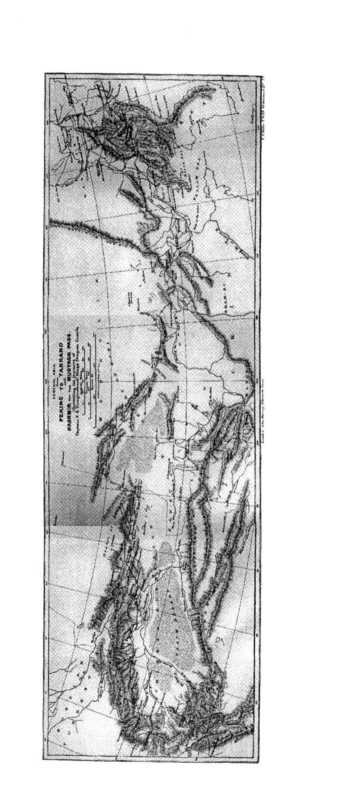

INDEX.

LONDON:
PRINTED BY WILLIAM CLOWES AND SONS, LIMITED,
STAMFORD STREET AND CHARING CROSS.

CPSIA information can be obtained at www.ICGtesting.com
Printed in the USA
BVOW02s1449161013

333919BV00001B/54/A